PAINTI.... ......

... A Rock & Roll Doctor's Tale.

All the best Linda

Love Steph

Stephen John Hartley   12/12/17

PAINTING SNAILS

... A Rock & Roll Doctor's Tale.

written and illustrated by
STEPHEN JOHN HARTLEY

ELI PRESS
Burnley

First edition 2017

Published by ELI PRESS, Burnley – part of Eli Records (UK).
www.elirecords.co.uk

Text and illustrations © Stephen Hartley 2017.

ISBN 978-1-9998114-0-2

For the not-muses and the muses.

This is an account based around the annual cycle of an allotment and includes tales of: playing in Rock & Roll bands; making records; an engineering apprenticeship; keeping an old van on the road, and more. It's all about peering between the cracks and challenging the norm – doing things your own way without necessarily toeing the line.

To produce a book, you're supposed to have an agent, an editor, a proofreader, a publisher and so on. I didn't bother with all that – I just did it, albeit with a bit of help and advice from my brother and a few friends.

'You should do a writing course.'
'You should read lots.'
'More detail.'
'Get rid of the swearing.'
'Keep the swearing.'
'Show, don't tell.'

I don't have time to read and I don't fancy a writing course so it's turned out the way it is – raw, spiky, disjointed and vernacular – just the way it's meant to be.

1. A big Idea

**Table, top of ranch – 1.43pm.
A Saturday in late September.**

It's my birthday. I'm on the ranch. The Met Office promised a barbecue summer so of course it's pissed down for the last couple of months. We've had a reprieve over the last week with hot dry weather. Today it's gloriously sunny – Indian summer with the first sniff of autumn.

There's a rough gnarled track that goes under the railway bridge at the top of the rows of terraced houses on the Yorkshire edge of town. It runs up through the allotments (known as 'the pens')* then bears right to more rows of terraces. It's only 15 minutes' walk from the town centre. The pens are an archaic reminder of when it was common for ordinary working people to keep pigeons, dogs, ferrets,

---

* Not the same thing as council allotments which are a much tamer beast.

hens, horses, etc. Most towns had pens once. These days a lot of them have gone – snatched up by greedy property developers and town planners.

The track rises high above the town and at the top, as it veers right, you can work out where it used to drop down towards the old cattle market. Clearly it was a packhorse trail. The view is magnificent, spanning the whole town. Dotted villages and farms rise up in the distance. Turn left and walk a hundred yards and there are two eighteenth-century farmhouses. They both have dates carved above their front doors. One has the initials GHE arranged in a triangle followed by a cross and the date 1777.

The other has a wonderful ornate stone panel above the lintel with two carved supports and a detailed patterned border. Arranged vertically down the centre are two cherubic faces separated by a Greek-style urn. Either side of the urn, the date 1748 is carved. The craftsmanship is amazing. There must be some cryptic significance in all those details. As a boy my dad remembered being forced to pay sixpence for a hen that his lurcher killed when he was walking through the same farmyard. He also remembered the pens. There were a lot more of them in those days – smaller ones – more gardens and pigeon coops.

I saw a sweet documentary a few years ago about an old bloke who had a smallholding. He called it his ranch and I pinched the idea. My ranch is a scruffy sloping rectangle of scrubland. It's about a tenth of an acre which is big for an allotment and it's more than enough for me to maintain. I'm sitting at the top where I've made a flat area of concrete and a pair of gates so that I can drive my van on from the sloping track. I made a little table especially for writing. A gentle breeze ruffles the hedge and sparrows, magpies and blackbirds flit about. I catch that musty autumnal smell in the air. There's a match on. You can see the top of the terrace from here. Every time they score, a *na naa na na, na naa na na* goes up from the crowd.

I don't read gardening books. I just try things out and see how they work. I started off with spectacular success rates approaching zero and now things are improving. Every year there's a bit more. I've worked out a simple method and it seems to be working. I could write a book about it – *Kenton Dunt's self-sufficiency method: A way of life*.

My mum had a friend called *Ron Freethy* who wrote a book – *From Agar to Zenry*. It's about his grandmother's vast knowledge of plants and their uses. He called her *The Little Witch*. There must be a lot of lost knowledge and undiscovered uses of plants. I'm interested in all that. They recently made an anti-cancer drug from yew and somebody won a Nobel Prize for isolating an anti-malarial drug from *Artemisia annua,* which is closely related to our native wormwood.

Modern society seems to have taken the emphasis away from walking out of the front door and knowing where to look for food and medicine. People live a lot longer these days so something in our medical system must be working but maybe we've become over-reliant on manufactured chemicals?

At the age of fourteen, I surprised my mum and dad by patiently transforming our tired neglected back garden. I re-dug the strawberry patch and of all things, I planted dahlias. I planted peas down the side of the garage. There was something comforting about gardening for a troubled teenager.

After my mum left school, she was a chemist at Parkinson's Pills. She was into science and loved nature. My dad was a founding member of the local caving club and in his youth, he spent all his spare time out and about in the Yorkshire Dales. It's not surprising then, that I'm interested in plants and addicted to being outside.

Whenever you tell someone that you have an allotment, often one of the first things that they say is, 'Have you got a shed?' It's that typical stereotypical view of blokes on allotments having sheds for refuge.

I ought to have a shed. I just haven't quite got round to it yet. Behind me is a neat concrete base which is about ten feet long and less than three feet wide. It nestles against the top boundary, close to the hedge. It has brick walls and a tiny fireplace but no roof, door or windows.

I built the back wall using little green bottles. It looks great when the sun shines through. I call it *demi-shed A*. I started it a few years ago but never got round to finishing it. It's supposed to be my writing shed.

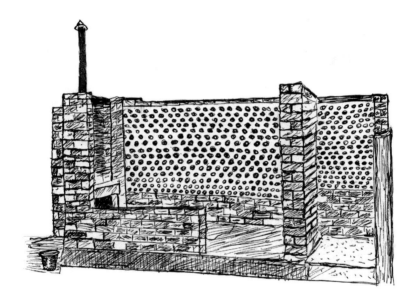

Diagonally across to my right is a half-shed with a flat roof, partial walls and a floor but no door or windows. It's about ten feet long and six feet wide. That's *Demi-shed B*. It has a little wood-burning stove in the corner made out of an old gas bottle. There's an old camping gas stove in the other corner and there's a green plastic box filled with basic utensils for cooking. There's a nice decking patio out front which is a late afternoon sun trap in summer.

Other projects invariably take precedence over shed completion but at least I can stay dry in Demi-shed B when it rains – before I built it, I just got wet, or sheltered under a sheet of polythene. I don't mind being in the rain. I get restless if I'm indoors for too long, particularly in windowless rooms.

I've had the ranch a good few years now and I've done quite a bit so far. When I first got it, there was nothing apart from a ramshackle goat shelter behind where I'm sitting. The fence was in tatters and right in the middle was a rather macabre mound of decomposing dead goats left behind by the previous tenant. I built a brazier next to it and slowly burned them. I repaired the fence bit by bit using anything I could find – pallet wood, old bed frames and so on. Whenever anyone comes to visit for the first time, I explain to them that everything that they can see down to the last square centimetre was built or planted by me. It never quite sinks in though. There's invariably a pause then they'll look at the stone steps leading to the top or the well or the big fireplace or one of the demi-sheds and say, 'did you build that?'

I'm not a natural gardener. I prefer building and making things. I'm forever snuffling about, planning paths and walls and knocking together timber to make propagators and sections of unfinished sheds and greenhouses. I've had no training in building or joinery, but my dad was an engineer and he could make anything. Some of it must have rubbed off on me and my brother. So much so, that I ended up doing an old-fashioned engineering apprentice-ship of the kind that doesn't really exist any more. My brother Michael is a cabinetmaker and he can turn his hand to most things.

The ranch runs roughly north to south with a wonderful view over the town and the big hills to the north-east and north-west. It's about three times longer than it is wide and slopes downwards. There's a thick hedge around it – mainly hawthorn, plus holly, ivy, hazel, blackthorn, wild rose and rowan. In summer it's completely private. When I started out, I used traditional gardening methods. Latterly, I've tweaked things and now I don't dig any more – I just put a layer of compost on top of the beds every winter. I don't believe in killing things, so by default it's all organic.

In front of the hedge is a border housing all the fruit trees and bushes. There's a fig tree at the bottom that does very well. The central area gets the maximum amount of light although there's some shading from trees to the south and west. There are three long beds running top to bottom broken into roughly four foot squares by raised brick walls and concrete paths. That's where the veg go. I'm obsessed with the best use of light and space. The bits that are cultivated stay cultivated and the rest stays wild. Even at its best it looks like a scruffy weed patch.

It turns out that what I'm doing is pretty close to permaculture – the gardening method that emulates natural ecosystems in order to grow things efficiently on a long-term basis.

There's a saying in Buddhism – 'As above, so below.' Principles working on a small scale can be extrapolated to bigger things. There are lots of lessons to be learned from this little rectangle of land on this scrubby hillside. It's a little microcosm of nature. All the clues are here. Whatever it is, something feels right. It feels good. It's OK to potter away and grow plants and a bit of food. It's my quiet revolution.

When John Peel died I felt compelled to do something as a gesture so I wrote a little tribute and sent it to a magazine. They published it. I told the tale of being alone on my birthday and feeling sorry for myself. I'd emailed him and he played me a record – best birthday present ever. John Peel was the radio DJ who championed countless new bands, becoming an icon and a hero to thousands of musos worldwide. He was a major part of my life – a massive influence. He was the backdrop to countless evenings over the years. I would often switch his programme on just to hear the sound of his voice. There was something common-sense, humanitarian, down-to-earth and levelling about him. The tribute was an exercise in the discipline of writing something and submitting it. Getting it published was a bonus. I got a lot of complementary emails and after that I thought, 'I could have a go at writing a book.'

I've been half-arsedly dabbling with writing for years. I once entered a writing competition at *Metro Books* in Bury and won a runner-up prize. I wrote a short story called *Tales of John The Dog*. It was about a dog that was actually an intelligent being from another planet and could talk. It was a pile of shite. I suspect that mine was the only entry so they gave me a five pound book token.

Last summer I went on a road trip in the van with the idea of writing a book. I wrote about a hundred pages. My plan was to write a part road trip, part anecdotal rambling tale, but it kind of fizzled out.

The trip was actually supposed to be our summer holiday. I booked three weeks off work and we planned to drive round the Scottish highlands. Unfortunately we got the dates of the school holidays wrong and it turned out that the lads were still at school for the first of my three weeks off. Oops. The idea was that they would come and join me in Inverness.

When I triumphantly reached Inverness (quite an achievement for a forty-five year old jalopy – the van that is, not me), I excitedly phoned home. It quickly became clear that the anarchic joy created by my absence was far more appealing to them than driving round Scotland in a bread bin on wheels. Oh well. I headed north *tout seul*. I drove round the highlands and finally reached John O' Groats. It was warm and sunny. I camped on a little site that looked north towards the Orkneys.

I never finished that book but the seed of the idea was sown – anecdotal ramblings against the framework of a road trip. That's a great idea for someone who travels a lot, but I don't. Even going to Manchester is a big adventure and if I'm away for more than three days I get serious ranch withdrawal symptoms. Instead, I thought of doing anecdotal ramblings within the framework of the annual allotment cycle with maybe a list of goals thrown in for good measure. That's it. That's the big idea.

I'll write a book from birthday to birthday – maybe I'll set myself a list of goals – finish the book (obviously); sort out that work/life balance conundrum; make that record; do a plant sale from the back of my old van; build a guitar amplifier.

Follow the path with a heart – that's my motto.
Right – let's go.

2. Engineering Days

Table, top of ranch. Sunday – 11.25am.

It's sunny again – balmy autumnal English sunshine. I'm gazing at the view over to the north-east. I can never get bored of it. The sky is always different. The light is always different. The vista rises to a gentle rolling horizon topped by a bowler-hat hill and sweeping moorland below it. You can make out white dotted farms towards the summit and pick out pinpoint cars on distant roads. Where are they going?

The trees in the allotment directly below mine have got pretty big and when they're in leaf, they blank out the view of the town centre. In winter, you can make out the straight mile of the canal through the leafless branches. The hedge seems to have grown more than ever this summer – eight feet tall, thick and lush. Pruning it is a huge job and takes weeks. I generally start at the beginning of November and try and finish it before spring. I used to end up with a huge pile of clippings, but now I either burn them, turn them into compost or dry them for firewood. I cut the thicker hawthorn into little loglets. It's amazing how much firewood comes from that hedge.

Last year I built a big fireplace – it looks like an old-fashioned lime kiln and represents the pinnacle of my building endeavours to date. The inside is curved like an old vaulted cellar. I made the formwork from willow and matchboard tongue and groove. I have a vague notion to incorporate an oven into the top and some kind of system for sterilising compost. The top side of the fireplace continues into a sloping retaining bottle wall which is at the same height as the hard standing at the top. I'm slowing filling in the space behind the wall with soil to

extend the flat concrete area. The fireplace has a short chimney which doesn't work that well, but once the fire gets going it's like a furnace and is perfect for shoving on the smaller hedge prunings.

Through the straggling tops of the hedge I can just make out the caravan place down the hill. Above that I can recognise all the streets on the east side of town including the main road that passes close to our house.

I love the English weather. Complaining about it is a national pastime. Every month, there's a superlative headline in the papers:

'The worst winter on record.' 'The worst flash floods this century.' 'The hottest summer since grandad's balls dropped.'

It's known to be damp round here – hence the cotton mills. It's grey and rainy quite a lot but in the context of a changing climate, I think ours is one of the best. There are still plenty of sunny days.

Today, I've gathered up some provisions and bought a paper. I'm having a long leisurely breakfast – home-made jam on toast, followed by coffee, followed by more of the same. My chair and writing table are strategically placed to command the best of the view. Sparrows are chattering and the crows survey their territory from the top of the tall ash in Linda's allotment over to my left.

Yesterday was a good birthday. We had a gig in the evening at *The Shooters*. I've played in bands since I was sixteen. Last night we played a mixture of covers and originals – mainly rock & roll and rockabilly with the odd bit of post-punk thrown in. I'm going to give up playing covers at some point and stick to doing my own stuff. When I got the notion to start writing, I bought a laptop. It's too bright up here to see the screen though, so I'm writing by hand and I'll type it up later.

When my dad left school, it was easy to get jobs. He just went to the sheet metal factory where his mate was working and got a job as a labourer. He didn't last long. To his embarrassment, his dad came and dragged him out and forced him to take on an engineering apprenticeship which was far less well paid. He went on to teach handicrafts and so had access to a workshop. He was always making bits and pieces for his boats and he made a lovely hexagonal chess table out of different coloured woods. His old engineering toolbox was in the cupboard under the stairs at the old house. Now it's on a purpose-built shelf in my back room. Michael and I were often accused of losing his tools. There were always tools about so making things was kind of in the blood.

I didn't like school much. It was pretty miserable at times. I got to do my A levels a year early as part of some stupid scheme at the grammar school. My dad understandably wanted me to have a better start than he had, and he had the idea that I would apply to engineering firms for university sponsorship.

I had other ideas. For a start, I was a guitarist in a punk band. I just couldn't do the A levels. I wasn't interested. I was going to all these interviews not even knowing what they were for. In the end, desperate to get my dad off my back, I responded to an advert in the paper which said: 'Wanted: person interested in engineering.' I got the job. It was a small traditional engineering firm housed in an old building that had previously been a fish market. There was an upstairs gallery that housed the offices. We made conveyor belt components for the brewery industry.

It was scary at first. The blokes there were pretty down-to-earth. They were into car rallying and motocross and they turned their hand to anything: building engines; repairing the fork lift truck; mending the factory roof. If something needed doing, they just did it.

The boss was a quiet unassuming chap and didn't say a lot to me. At the beginning he said that he had no sons and that he wanted me to carry on the firm. At the time, that didn't mean a thing to a shy seventeen year old. It was only years later that I realised he probably meant it. Some of the blokes referred to him as *Nobtosser*. I've never heard that particular vernacular expletive before or since but it's sort of made its way into our family pantheon over the years and by rights I should be credited with bringing it into the English language[*].

I remember making my first ever washer on a lathe. A little circular thing with a hole in the middle – it was pretty rough but I was pleased with it. I showed it to Grahame, the toolmaker who was supervising me. He looked at it with mock incredulity then threw it over his shoulder. I began by learning how to run the injection moulding machines then I was taught how to use the lathes, milling machines and grinder. The job sort of progressed into a formal apprenticeship and I went away to training school in the second year. I did well and won two prizes. I should have got apprentice of the year but they said I had an unfair advantage because I'd already done a year so they gave it to someone else.

---

[*] I'll be liaising with the Oxford English Dictionary presently.

When I came back, we'd moved to a factory on the edge of open countryside. I think they were kind of proud of me and they treated me a bit differently. I'd also passed my driving test and got my first car. The tool-room had a big pair of double doors that we opened in the summer. At the back, there was open countryside. As factories went, it was one of the nicest.

There was a kind bloke at work called Jack. He looked out for me. If I accidentally knocked off one of the teeth of a cast-iron sprocket when I was trying to straighten it up in the lathe chuck, I'd go to him. 'Er Jack...' A bit later he'd walk by with a sack of rubbish and wink. 'Your sprocket's in the bottom of this sack.' Sadly, he died of bladder cancer. It was my first experience of somebody close dying. His wife gave me his tools.

I'm still good friends with the foreman Max. He's a wonderful character full of sparkling wit. He was always playing practical jokes on the boss. He's over seventy now and he's still working. He has a little workshop and I visit him once in a while. I went the other week to ask him if he would weld a bracket for me off a trolley that I use on the ranch. 'There you go', he said, pointing to the arc welder.

It's many years since I've done any welding and it came back to me as if it was yesterday – a good omen for repairing my van. I got a big thrill out of it.

When I finished my apprenticeship the other two tool-makers left to set up their own business. I was desperately restless and I had wanderlust. I was getting lots of ideas about living outside the rat race and I didn't want to pay for the boss's next BMW so I left.

I bought a tent and camping equipment. My dad drove me to the M6 and off I went hitch-hiking to France. The boss thought that because we'd all left together, I'd gone with the other two and that I'd lied to him. He only believed me when I sent him a postcard.

I wrote a song about my apprenticeship *(Engineering Days)*. It's on one of the *Vincent Black Lightning* records. I recorded it at the old house on a *Tascam Portastudio*. I played everything on it myself. It's one of my favourite recordings. I recorded the sound of an angle grinder on the back step to drown out the vernacular first line. (Otherwise it wouldn't have got any radio airplay). The vocals are recorded through my Vox distortion pedal. As the song says, the apprenticeship set me up for life.

Hence fixing cars, building sheds and so on kind of come naturally. I like to imagine the design of something in my head and just make it without having to draw it. For ages I didn't even have a tape measure up here – just a spirit level. I try and design things to be utterly functional and minimalist – purpose-built to complement the space – no frills. The Chinese have a name for that kind of thing. I'm slowly building raised beds, paths, sheds, greenhouses and so on.

The apprenticeship was a good foundation in how to live independently. If something broke you fixed it. Those engineering principles of starting off with rough chunks of steel and making something very precise can be applied to anything. When I started, I had zero confidence. When I came out, I'd been taught a practical way of life inspired by some pretty impressive role models. I had a good livelihood and I had my own car. That's what I call a good education. The wisdom and experience of the old passed onto the young. Simple. A lot of today's higher education system is bollocks. Kids are tricked into obscene amounts of debt in exchange for poorly-taught courses that have little chance of providing them with a worthwhile livelihood.

We're conditioned to believe that we have to acquire a lot of what we need from an 'official' source when in fact a large proportion can be done DIY – making records, growing food, conveyancing, bartering – side-stepping the stranglehold that global institutions have on our lives. Less is more and so on.

Marrying sound engineering principles with nature continues to have endless possibilities. In fact careful observation teamed with the innovative use of technology is one of the central principles of permaculture. I could use the wind to grind flour? I could use the sun to make electricity to run a battery-powered tractor?

Steady on boy. Steady on.

3. Rock & Roll

The summer has suddenly gone. Now it's wet, cold and windy. I've been up the ranch today tidying and pottering. It was too wet to sit and write.

If you're seriously into allotmenteering, there's always something to do. There are the part-timers who grow a few veg when the weather is good then there are the rain-and-shiners like me. An allotment is for life, not just for spring and summer. Once you make the decision that growing your own food is a worthwhile thing to do, there's no turning back. There are a string of jobs that need doing regularly – horse shite to shift, hedges to prune, fences to maintain and of course regular planting.

I'm still bringing home a decent amount of food at this time of year: potatoes (stored in sawdust); onions; carrots (grown in tubs on the roof of demi-shed B to protect them against carrot fly); leeks; figs; apples; kale; sweetcorn and courgettes.

I'm beginning to tidy the beds that are finished with for the season. Plants that have died back just stay in the ground. I trim them down to ground level then mulch with a layer of fresh manure. I watched a fascinating documentary that explained the value of leaving the roots of expired plants in the ground and growing cover crops such as clover and brassicas to protect the soil. The roots are colonised by fungal mycelia, helping to improve the soil, giving it good drainage and water-retaining properties. Clovers of course are also nitrogen fixing. I don't know how well it will work up here in the long term because this is the first year that I've tried it.

I get an endless supply of horse muck from my neighbour Linda. The track separates our allotments. She's been up here since she was a little girl. She knows a lot about horses and is an astute business woman. She has two ponies and a semi-feral cat – she has an arena, teaches riding and helps out as a steward at shows. The horses produce a lot of manure and it's the lifeblood of the ranch. You need a lot of organic material for this kind of gardening. I've built a midden into my fence and Linda just mucks out directly into it. You're supposed to leave it to rot for a couple of years, especially as the manure is woodchip-based (as opposed to straw) but I put it directly onto the ground. It has a number of advantages. For a start it's sterile in that there are no weed seeds or slug and snail eggs in it. Secondly, it's warm. Within weeks, earthworms appear and after a couple of months, plants seem to grow fine in it. It's all about experimenting up here.

I remember reading a feature in one of the Sunday papers along the lines of 'Rock stars and their allotments.' Ha. No relevance to me - I'm an unrock notstar.

My first band once supported *The Clash* at King George's Hall. That was pretty exciting but nowhere near as exciting as when I 'bought' the ranch. At that time the land was owned by a chap in Morecambe - we didn't actually own our allotments. People traded them for a couple of hundred quid, but still had to pay rent every year (about nine quid). We eventually got the chance to buy them. That's a long story - almost a book in itself.

When we supported them, The Clash were in their white-man-reggae phase with Mickey Dread in tow. I never liked them. They seemed a bit uppity and snobbish to me. OK, they were an accomplished live band, but their working class kids' preaching didn't ring true given Woody's upbringing.

I had an inspirational moment when I was fourteen. I'd recorded some Beatles songs on my little cassette player at my friend John Griffiths' house. I was listening back to them and I had a bit of a joyous epiphany when *Eight Days a Week* came on. I thought, 'yes – this is what I want to do – I want to be in a band and write songs.'

That Christmas I got a ¾-size classical guitar and I played it endlessly. Status Quo's *Down Down* single was in the charts and I bought it. I adored the guitar intro - especially the riff after the first jangly bit. I spent hours trying to learn it and that's how I mastered bar chords. Our friends Peter and Roger lived a few doors up the road from us. Roger was a year older than me and Peter was a year younger – my brother's age. We'd been to nursery together and we were at the same school. One of my earliest memories is being taken to nursery by their mum in a red Morgan.

One hot summer's day, a couple of years before I got my guitar, Roger and I were sprawled on our back street listening to his little transistor radio. We were a bit bored – it was roasting. I remember vividly the tarmac on the pavement, which was a kind of russet red, with little flecks of white in it - I've never ever seen that colour of pavement anywhere since. The street itself was still cobbled and in between the cobbles was black tar which became soft when it was hot. We used to pull it up and mould it into little balls. A record came on the radio that grabbed us both. It was strange and exotic, so much so that I was a bit embarrassed for liking it. I had a strange yearning to hear it again. It was *Metal Guru by* T-Rex. It grabbed me hook, line and sinker. I was too young to have the wherewithal to buy records, so I listened to the radio a lot. We all watched top of the pops which was an uncomfortable experience at our house due to my dad's ranting at the various 'ponces' on the screen. I did have one record. I'd bought it at a jumble sale with my mum a few weeks earlier. It was *Funny Funny* by the Sweet. We had an old radiogram in the back room and a big pile of 78s. I used to love playing them just for the novelty of working the record player. They were mostly classical but there was *Oft in the stilly night* and *Beneath my window (Oh solo meo)*. My mum and dad had one Peter Sellers single – that was the extent of our family musicality.

I got more and more interested in music and my guitar playing was slowly coming on. Roger had a classmate called *Simon Wilkinson* who was a fantastic piano player. He was tall and handsome with red curly hair. I once went with Roger to his house. They had a grand piano and Simon played Meade Lux Lewis's *Honky Tonk Train Blues* – the *Emerson, Lake and Palmer* version was in the charts at the time. I was completely blown away. We had a piano at home but we'd bashed it up as kids and half the notes didn't work. I was so inspired that I fixed it. I painstakingly glued all the broken hammers and dislodged wooden levers. My mum got it tuned and I was off. I learned *The Entertainer, Maple Leave Rag, Fur Elise, Moonlight Sonata* and finally I started learning *Honky Tonk Train Blues*. I think Roger was inspired too. He got a *Welson* electric piano.

It was the time of prog rock and Roger and Simon and their mates were listening to Gong, Wishbone Ash, ELP, PFM * and so on. Prog wasn't my cup of tea – I just didn't like it. We all listened to John Peel. He had a late-night slot on Radio one and played anything and everything. As ever, he championed the new and the exciting, the fresh and the unusual. When punk came in, he embraced it immediately and wholeheartedly.

Punk was a fresh blast that blew away the cobwebs of the diarrhoeic self-indulgent twiddly-diddly prog rock bilge that was around at the time. It was a two-fingered salute to the rock establishment.

Several hippies got haircuts and hid their prog records under their beds – Johnny Rotten and his *Faust* collection to name but one. Some of them hid their middle class public schoolboy roots and set themselves up as punk icons. They never fooled me. I thought that they were all

* Italian prog band affectionately re-christened *Pack o' Fuckin Masturbators*.

hypocrites. They were spouting anti-establishment rebellion but hold on a minute, weren't they all signed to major labels? CBS, EMI, Virgin and so on. Most of them came from accomplished rock bands. They just changed their image when the record companies saw the commercial potential of the punk movement.

Nevertheless, there was an independent subversive element to punk. The first wave of music industry engineered bands inspired ordinary working class kids to go out and do it themselves – write fanzines and make their own records – create new fashion from charity shop finds. That's when it got interesting. Especially up North. That was our backdrop.

Roger and I decided to form a punk band. We started playing together and writing songs. I wrote *Gutter Girl* and *Heart Attack* and we wrote *Death to Disco* together. After that, he wrote most of the songs.

My brother Michael briefly joined us on guitar and later went on to form *Chimp Eats Banana* with Boff and a few others. Chimp Eats Banana started off as a non-existent band as part of an elaborate schoolboy joke. At school there were lots of Stephens so Roger started calling me *Saitch* based on my initials. Michael got called *Maitch* which quickly developed into *Midge*. Saitch became *Sage*.

Michael was a superb climber and jokingly got called a chimp. The joke went one step further when schoolmates Boff and Dan sent a mysterious parcel to school addressed to him. He was promptly summoned to the headmaster's office.

'What's going on Hartley?'

'Er, I don't know.'

'Better be careful,' said supercilious chemistry teacher *Bernie Grime*. 'It might be a bomb.'

It was actually a bunch of bananas in a shoebox.

For the next stage of the joke, Dan started sending non-existent Chimp Eats Banana gig notices to the NME gig guide. The band was subsequently formed on the strength of the name alone – Michael, Boff, Dan, Khany, Gilly, Hopper, Tommy and Roger's brother Peter. We all went to The Grammar School.

They released a cassette album called *Cardboard Box* which was packaged in shoeboxes from Khany's dad's shoe shop. They did a brilliant one-off gig one night at *The Inn Place* as *Grooveline* where they did piss-take covers of crap 70s songs in a smoochy Frank Sinatra style. The highlight was *Tie a Yellow Ribbon round the Old Oak Tree*.

Someone sprayed 'Midge is a chimp' in the bus shelter just down from our house. A whole bunch of us hung around the park, generally making nuisances of ourselves much to the disdain of the local residents.

After a few weeks the council painted the bus shelter. The day after someone sprayed 'MIDGE IS STILL A CHIMP' right across the back. Everyone on the bus could see it. It made the local paper.

I first met Boff when we both started at The Grammar School. He was tall and had a basin haircut. We were both doing art O level – he was sitting at the back of the class. The teacher, *Willy Lonsdale,* said something pompous and patronising then sloped off into his office at the front of the classroom. Boff threw a two-fingered salute in the air and I thought, 'there's someone on my wavelength.' We both got Saturday jobs at *Supasave* which was across from the bus station. At the time Boff wore round glasses and the foreman called him a boffin – I abbreviated it to Boff and it stuck.

After a few promising rehearsals in his attic, Roger and I started looking round for a singer. *Quentin Termite* was a potential candidate but in the end we chose Kev Hemingway. He was the first person at our school to bleach his hair and get a proper 'punk' haircut. He looked the part. His brother-in-law was a drummer and there was the possibility of getting a drum kit given.

There was a cocky lad called Haggis who wore a duffle coat and hung around the park with us. He reckoned that he could sing so he joined us and then we were a proper band. Kev moved onto cardboard boxes pending the arrival of the drum kit. Roger bought a Kawai synthesiser and played the bass lines on it with one hand and his Welson piano with the other. I remember nervously lying awake at night thinking how difficult it would be to make ourselves heard. There were thousands of bands out there trying to be successful.

Boff had his finger on the pulse when it came to music. We went on a school trip to London and he knew all the places to go. We went to *Rough Trade* and bought *Sniffin Glue* fanzine which came with a free flexi-disc of ATV's *Love Lies Limp*. We used to buy obscure and collectable records at *The Record Exchange* and sell them in *Melody Maker*. One day Boff spotted a tiny advert in *Sounds* *. It was for *The North West Musicians Collective* which was based at *North West Arts* on King St in Manchester. They had a band night every Tuesday at *Band on The Wall*. If you went to a few meetings you could get a gig. Haggis, Boff and I went along on the bus. We all fancied Louise, the girl who ran it.

---

* Sounds started off as a bit of a heavy rock music weekly, but it embraced punk before the NME and Melody Maker so became the first choice for punk fans.

Our first gig was at *Central Methodist youth Club*. It was packed. It was clear that Haggis was a great front man. He had the charisma and the moves. After that I rang up every single working men's club in town trying to get gigs. We had no concept of what was a suitable music venue. Working men's clubs and pubs were the only places that had 'live music' on as far as we knew. No-one wanted us but I persisted and finally a conservative club down the road agreed to put us on. We had to do an audition. The rotund concert secretary asked us if we knew any David Soul... we didn't. On the night of the gig they wouldn't let our mates in because they were all under-age. My guitar strap came off during the first song (*Freedom*). We got chucked off after two songs.

We had four covers in our set – *All or nothing* by Little Bob Storey taken from the *New Wave* album (we'd never heard of the Small Faces at that time), the Kinks' *Where Have all the Good Times gone,* the Adverts' *One Chord Wonders* and *Runaway* by Slaughter and the dogs. I think they're the only covers we ever did.

The Borough was our local (even though Haggis, Kev and I were under-age). That's where we met Gary Pickles who was a regular there. We unkindly dubbed him *Tubby Pickles*. When we'd been chucked off, he stood up for us and insisted that the concert secretary pay us. He was our hero for the night. He came to all our early gigs. He wasn't our manager as such, but he was part of our inner circle. He's there with us on the clumsily drawn flimsy paper cover of the first version of our album.

Band on The Wall was our first 'proper' gig. There were 3 bands on. We were on first. I can't remember who was on second – it might have been *The Spherical Objects*. A couple of weeks earlier Boff and I had picked up a 12" single in Manchester by *Jon The Postman*. It was in a brown paper bag. Mark E Smith did a guest appearance on it. I wish I still had it. It was on Bent records. Boff had the bright idea to write to Jon and invite him to our gig at Band on The Wall. We wrote him a wacky letter all decorated in coloured felt tip.

The excitement of having a gig in MANCHESTER was immense. My brother organised a coach and again they wouldn't let our fans in because they all looked too young. Jon turned up and brought along Dave Bentley, the bloke who owned Bent records. They liked us and offered to put a single out. That's how we got started. Buzzcocks' Steve Diggle was there. He had a blue Morris Minor. The last band on were *The Frantic Elevators*. The bassist played a Hofner violin bass through a Vox cab. The drummer was ace and had a neat little black Ludwig kit. The guitarist had a black Les Paul copy and played spiky chopped chords. The singer had cropped red hair and was awesome. I could say that they were the best band that I'd ever seen but actually they were the only band I'd ever seen.* I loved them, although they didn't quite fit into the Manchester punk scene. They were a bit before their time. They did a one-note song called *Production Prevention* that stuck in my memory. I was sick in the back of the van on the way home – all over Roger's keyboard – too much to drink.

As a bonus, the gig was reviewed in Sounds by Mick Middles. We got a really good write-up and The Elevators got a right slating – he compared them to a mini Status Quo on a bad night. We thought it was hilarious. Their singer was furious.

We went on to do quite a few gigs with them and they became my favourite band. There's a fantastic bootleg of them playing at *Devilles* which is one of my top five albums. They recorded four singles and the last one is by far the best – deffo in my top ten singles. After they split, the singer formed a middle-of-the-road soul band. They recorded a version of the Elevators last single which shot up the charts.

We recorded *Death to Disco* for our first single at Cargo studios in Rochdale. Cargo was cheap and during its heyday as the post-punk movement burgeoned, it was busy

---

* Not quite true – I'd seen *Eater* at Bold Street Working Men's Club a few weeks earlier.

twenty four hours a day. The owner John Brierley did the day shift and engineer Colin Richardson did the night shift. Lots of well-known bands recorded there. John Peel played the single and we were off. That was out first break. We were still a four-piece then. A short time later, we poached Gary Brown, the bass player from local rivals *The Pathetix*. We kidnapped him and took him to The Borough and got him sloshed.

One night we played a gig at *The Union* in Colne. We were getting pretty popular locally and it was packed. We could hardly play for the crowd surging forward. It was one of our best gigs. That's where I met Inger. I'd decided it was time I had a girlfriend so I used some ham-fisted chat-up lines after reading about a successful chatter-up of women in The Daily Mirror. I must have been making an impression because she asked me if I'd like to walk her home. She was pretty with short blonde hair. I liked her name.

'Er no thanks. We have to get the gear in the van.' I was so slow and stupid. That would have been that, but she rang me up a week later and we went to *The Railway Workers*. It turns out we had the same birthday. I was a year older.

The Railway Workers was a working men's club in Nelson. They let us use the upstairs function room and it became the venue for the north-east Lancs punk scene.

Spider and Quent ran it and it thrived. There were bands on every weekend and Spider was the coolest DJ playing all the latest punk. We played there a few times, as did Crass and The Fall.

At the end of the Union gig, we were approached by a bearded chap with afro hair and dungarees. He was carrying a clipboard. He was a flamboyant hippy type – very posh. He told us he was a *Theatre Fellow* at the local arts association. He gave us a very impressive spiel and said that he could help us out. His name was Simon.

We were so young and clueless that he could have said anything and we would have believed him. His poshness and his charismatic theatrical persona would serve us well in the months to come. Under his patronage, we made full use of the arts association facilities including their van, their PA, their guitars and amps, their office and telephone and their rehearsal space. We were stopped by the police on a few occasions on the way back from gigs. The arts association logo was painted on the side of the van so it looked quite official. Simon would give his best performance and come across as a high-ranking member of the elite.

'Good evening officer, just returning from a performance in Manchester.'
'Very good sir. Drive carefully now.'

The reality on the inside of the van was even more salubrious than the motorway scenes from *Withnail and I*. Simon was a right old hippy. He often used to say to me, 'Sage you're so fucking naïve man.' He was right of course. In fact we were all naïve but I was probably more naïve than most. Thankfully, Inger was pretty astute. She could see through bullshit that I wouldn't have spotted in a million years. On one occasion Simon lost the van keys after we'd loaded up all the gear. Inger suggested unloading to see if the keys were in the back. 'Don't patronise me love,' said Simon. Eventually we took all the equipment out again and there were the keys.

After the success of the single, Dave Bentley offered to do an album for us. We recorded it during the night (also at Cargo) because it was cheaper. Peel had also offered us a session which coincidentally was booked when we were recording the album. John Clarke, a dealer friend of Simon's from Rochdale offered to drive us down to London in his Luton van. He met us outside Cargo after a night's recording and we all piled in the back with our gear and drove to Maida Vale. Ploppy* as usual shoved everyone

---

* Nicknames and pseudonyms were very popular at the time of punk. Dan wrote a poem which appears on the album taking the piss out of Kev and his drums calling him *Ploppy*. Dan in turn had been given his nickname by Mr Waddington, an eccentric teacher at the junior school that we went to. He later became Danbert.

else out of the way and commandeered what he thought was the best spot – the cosy little area overhanging the cab. He was wrong.

John Clarke drove like a nutter and every time he accelerated forward as fast as he could, Ploppy was flung from his perch onto all the equipment below. He spent the trip to London wedging himself in as the rest of us snoozed peacefully.

Many years later, long after Cargo had shut down, there was a ceremony to unveil a blue plaque that had been put outside. There were various little events on throughout the day. Simon and I went. Roger was there too. John Brierley is now a cameraman and Colin Richardson who was the engineer for a lot of our recordings is now a successful producer in America. They were both there.

In another incident, we played at a battle of the bands competition at *The Cat's Whiskers* and we won it. Simon was one of the judges and another judge was *Billy Jacobs* who was a journalist for the local paper and was on our side. Fellow punk band *The Constipated Poodles* had tried to get in and had been refused entry by the bouncers. They really looked the part – Mohicans, safety pins and attitude to match. Simon charmed the bouncers in his usual posh way.

'Oh don't be fooled by appearances, they're the loveliest bunch of lads you could ever meet.'

Once inside, they trashed the dressing rooms and pulled all the wash-basins off the walls. When the management threatened to call the police, John Clarke took a thick wad of cash out of his pocket and paid for the damage.

The engineer for our Peel session was Dale Griffin, drummer with *Mott The Hoople*. I don't think he liked us. We were very childish and wasted time wrestling on the floor – very un-BBC. Most of the daft sketches between the tracks on the album came about from messing about in the back of the van travelling to gigs. The *Star-spotting* sketch was inspired after I heard a gardening programme on radio Lancashire with a very Northern sounding presenter, speaking in a rather slow deliberate voice. Haggis knew all the words to Don Maclean's *American Pie* and he would sing it all the way through. We joined in on the choruses. We also sang lots of other little ditties including *Barbara Ann* and 'Oh Pendle, oh Pendle, thou standest alone – twixt Burnley and Clitheroe, Whalley and Colne.'

The album did very well. We called it *Instant Classic*. It got good reviews in the music press. When the first issue on Bent Records sold out, we went back to Cargo and recorded a couple of different tracks and remixed the whole lot. We released the second version on *Snotty Snail*, the label that Simon was developing. Rough Trade distributed it and Boff painstakingly drew the iconic cover comprising hundreds of tiny figures in fine spidery black pen. The first issue is now pretty rare and is considered to be the best version. It has more daft bits on it.

We played quite a bit in Manchester and occasionally we would see famous people from bands like *The Buzzcocks* and *The Fall.* It was inconceivable to me that they might be there to see us. I always hoped that they would go before we played, because I was so self-conscious. I remember seeing Marc Riley (Fall bass player) at *The Cypress Tavern.* It was many years later that I learned that he had actually organised the gig and he was a fan. I was completely clueless about the organisational side of things – Simon sorted all that out, and we never saw a penny. I recall being thrilled at getting a brand new Vox distortion pedal from band money – I've still got it and I still use it. That's the only thing I ever got from the band. Fortunately, we had the sense to keep hold of all our royalty rights. (Although later Simon did roguishly try and claim them for himself and licensed our back catalogue to Cherry Red without telling us – it took Kev ages to get it all back in our names). Roger could so easily have said 'I'm the song-writer, I want a bigger share,' but we split everything equally five ways. What a testament to his modesty and humility.

I'm in Love with Margaret Thatcher was our second single. It was a throwaway three-chord ditty that Roger wrote on the night of the election. He came up with the line in the same way that Paul McCartney used *scrambled eggs* when he started writing *Yesterday*. The line morphed into a full song. We were never overtly political but we did have a naïve social astuteness.

We spotted an advert (again in Sounds) for a package deal which included recording, accommodation and a thousand singles with picture sleeves. We enquired and got a nice brochure which showed two *Smashy and Nicey* type figures in front of a roaring log fire which was actually in the studio. We had images of bedding down for the night in front of the fire after a successful day's recording.

The studio was in Market Drayton (coincidentally the birthplace of Haggis's girlfriend Deborah) and the label was *Redball*. Roger's dad lent us the money and drove us down. When we arrived there was indeed a big fireplace in part of the studio, but the fire wasn't lit. It quickly became apparent that our overnight accommodation was going to be elsewhere. I can't remember much about the actual recording, but the single did well and has successfully re-emerged since, so it must have gone OK. The 1000 Redball copies sold out quickly and we re-pressed it and released it on Snotty Snail. It turned out that our accommodation was a faded pale blue ramshackle shed in the middle of a wood.

We all got bitten by fleas. In the evening, Roger and I went out on the town. The last pub we went in was very bizarre. There were blokes with wigs and lipstick giving us funny looks. We got stopped by the police on the way back then woke up the occupants of a nearby house after their large dog heard us and went berserk. We ran through the woods in terror trying to find the shack, imagining the crazed hound at our heels.

At the height of our success, Sounds journalist Garry Bushell invented a sub-genre of punk called *Punk Pathetique* closely allied to another of his fabricated fuckwit genres *Oi*. He tried to include us in it. It was a movement of Southern thicko bands and I hated the idea. Roger wrote *Garry Bushell's Band of the Week* which is on the B-side of Thatcher. We did a telephone interview with Bushell and I told him plainly what I thought. Around the same time, Boff had the brilliant idea to do a piss-take song by a non-existent band called *Skin Disease*. It was called 'I'm Thick', and the only lyric is 'I'm Thick.' Bushell fell for it and included it on an 'Oi' EP released by Sounds.

As a band we were different. We were daft. We were irreverent. We were unfashionably anti-fashion. We were charmingly inept. We didn't ponce about. We didn't sell out. Although we never toured, we produced a body of work that was off the beaten track and way above average.

Roger is a great songwriter and there are a few wonderful pop songs in there. Maybe one day someone will recognise their worth and do a covers album. All in all we did an LP, four singles and a Peel session. Not bad for a bunch of feckless teenagers.

None of us can clearly remember how we chose our name but we all agree that it was based on a passing comment made by my dad about our attempts to look like a punk band. In years since, I've spent ages trying to think of good band names but I don't remember doing it back then. As we were all traipsing through our house one day, my dad said, 'You're not sensible,' and that was that. We spent ages finalising the exact detail of the spelling: *The Not Sensibles'*, *'Not Sensible'*, *'The Notsensibles'*

In the end we settled on NOTSENSIBLES without the the. We were pompously pedantic about people getting it right. What a great name. It was perfect. It fitted the punk ethic of the day and reflected our daft schoolboy irreverence and weird sense of humour.

My dad was a teacher and he used to bring home records from his pupils for us to sign. It's funny how our teenage memories filter out any parental involvement. They must have been involved, because we were too young to drive when we started. I do vividly remember going to buy my first electric guitar with my dad and Michael. New Hall

Street in Preston was littered with interesting junk shops and that's where we headed. I got a *Zenta*. It was red and SG-shaped and had lots of chrome. I was hugely excited. Gerry, the technician at my dad's work, adapted a reel-to-reel tape recorder so I could plug into it.

Michael decided that he also wanted an electric guitar so we went back to New Hall Street. I persuaded him that it would be more useful to buy an amplifier and we could then share and both play. We ended up with a grey rattling buzzing *Welson*. Shortly afterwards, we went back a third time and Michael got an *Antoria* guitar. It was salmon red/pink and vaguely Strat-shaped. He had it for several years. I think it ended up being sprayed green.

Notsensibles could never have lasted long; we had a certain haplessness about us, attracting fuck-ups at crucial moments. The full story would be a book in itself – *The unwinding road to un-rock & roll and back: NOTSENSIBLES, a memoir by Pendle Bifferton*. Inevitably, we split up after three action-packed years. A few years later, Boff, Dan and my brother had all moved to Leeds. They'd all been at the University. They dropped out and formed *Chumbawamba*. They were often asked how they got their name and they told a different story every time. The true story comes from Paris. They were all living in a squat in Armley and my brother and Graham Cardy from *The Mirror Boys* rebuilt an old bus. They drove round Europe in it, making money from busking. They saw a bizarre busker outside the Pompidou Centre. All he was doing was shuffling around a bunch of artefacts including a toilet. He was making strange mumbling noises. 'Chumbawamba' came from the sound of his mumbling. Funnily enough I saw the same busker on a different occasion when I was hitch-hiking round France. Michael played with them for four years, but he somehow manages to be written out of their history. They started as a 3-piece and expanded. They were more into the anarcho side of things than us and we kind of drifted apart.

After Notsensibles I didn't do much musically for a while, but my post-punk Rock & Roll ethic was well formed. I later spent five years as a busker. That DIY approach continued to be my great inspiration – doing as much as possible from a back room in the North of England. I love investigating things that can be done at home without relying on the 'system' and that philosophy is 100% applicable to the ranch.

The ranch is part of a way of life – it represents a little piece of freedom. Nature's cycles just happen – spring follows winter and so on. It's quite reassuring and very peaceful and there's always that hare-brained dream of running a smallholding and selling plants out of the back of an old van. It's also a quiet discipline that works towards a vision of independence – I have to believe that shifting several barrow-loads of horse muck on a freezing winter's day has a greater purpose.

Haggis is also a ranchero and Roger works for the parks. Allotments and Rock & Roll – what a fine combination.

4. Notes on Art and Language

I'm having to spend more and more time tapping into computers and staring at irritating screens. That darned internet is a double-edged sword. A lot of websites seem to have common themes, causing profound annoyance. Many normal people seem to cope well with it but I'm reduced to frustration. For a start, they want to extract all your personal information from you. 'You have not completed the required field.' Secondly, they make sure that they are impossible to contact and direct you to a page called *FAQs*. What the fuck are FAQs? They reckon that they're *Frequently asked questions* but they don't fool me. If they're impossible to contact in the first place how on earth can people frequently ask them questions? It's all bullshit.

Getting outside on the computerless ranch is a perfect antidote to these frustrations. I've actually invented the concept of *IAQs* – infrequently asked questions. They're questions that frankly, I should have been asked by now. You see interviews with successful people on telly where they're being asked lots of interesting questions. I get asked fuck all. 'What was going through your mind when you wrote that song?' 'What were your main influences during your green period?' 'What's your favourite film?' 'What's your favourite guitar?' I imagine myself being interviewed on telly by *Kirsty Wark* about my latest book and latest record. She's asking me non-stop IAQs.

Today, after doing the first section of hedge pruning, I've done some concreting. I do a lot of concreting. I mix it all by hand using the aluminium roof of an old Morris Traveller. Once upon a time, I drove Morris Minor vans and Travellers. The roof is the only remnant of a Traveller that I bought for spares years ago. I took down a section of fence and Linda helped me get it on. She drove it and I pushed. I have a cement mixer but I've hardly used it.

Flat areas of concrete are havens against the endless onslaught of weeds. Once an area is concreted, it's 'claimed' and I'll never have to weed it again. Some people go to the gym. I mix concrete and dig. It keeps me thin. I make a section of path at a time. In between the paths, I'm building square raised beds using brick. It works well. Each raised bed is about four foot square and surrounded by a path. It's very labour-intensive initially, but once a bed is made, it's low maintenance. The bricks are all ones that I've dug up, found or been given. I remember a friend of mine being asked at a job interview 'What would you do with a brick?' I wish I'd been asked that question at one of my interviews – they wouldn't have been able to shut me up. Bricks are quite interesting because they're mostly stamped with the brickworks where they were made: 'Deerplay'; 'Accrington'; 'Summit'; 'Enfield'. It's all clay round here so there were lots of brickworks including one known as *The Kilns* which was about fifteen minutes walk from here. There's a housing estate there now which has taken the name. Beryl lives there. There's a very ornate *Brickmakers* pub in town.

I rotate crops between the beds. The concept of rubbish on an allotment is non-existent. Everything is reusable. Even broken glass and rusty nails can be used as a base for areas of concrete. Non-degradables get burned. I'm always on the lookout for bits of timber and building materials. Looking in skips is one the great joys of the snuffling hunter-gatherer. Whenever I'm clearing new ground, I have three plastic sacks to hand and separate out brick and stone, glass & rusty nails (sharps) and anything that burns. I also keep anything decorative such as bits of broken pottery and incorporate them into walls and paths.

My dad used to live in Ainsdale and when we visited him, I loved beachcombing and picking up bits of coloured glass to incorporate into paths. I wore out the front suspension of the car teaching the kids to joyride on the beach (sand got in the joints).

Is there any place for art in allotmenteering? Of course there is. Nature is the greatest artist – pattern, symmetry and infinite palette – it's all there. Is language art? Song lyrics and poems, innit? Is there any point to all this art-fart stuff? Art is central to pretty much every culture and religion that ever existed so there must be something in it.

Maybe it's a spectrum? At one end there are the snivelling self-indulgent splatterers. That doesn't interest me. I reside at the other end with the misfits and don't-give-a-fucks who manage to produce something unique and beautiful in spite of and because of the surrounding shittiness.

I remember seeing a Bowie interview where he referred to art as the 'grey space in the middle', not complete until viewed by the consumer. 'The value of art is in the grey space between the creator and the perceiver.'

Notsensibles were were proud of our *Ain't been to no music school* * credentials. Music school and art school were distinctly uncool in our Northern punk rock world – they were for puffs and poshies. Punk was very snobby – everything that came before was shite – that's why all the newly formed punk bands hid their record collections. Funnily enough, ska and reggae were somehow exempt (and Ivor Cutler of course). They were cool.

A bit before punk arrived, I heard *Make yours a happy home,* by *Gladys Knight and The Pips* on the radio. I adored it but would never have dared admit it. I bought it from *Ames Records* in the market precinct. My heart was pounding in case someone I knew came in. I hid it under my coat.

I got interested in art through people like Boff and Inger. We learned about the pop artists. I read about The French Impressionists and how they came across Japanese prints which had been used in a similar manner to newspaper to wrap exported items. The impressionists were impressed by the prints and took a lot of influence from them. Me too. I started drawing and painting. As always, I stuck to

---

* *Ain't bin to music school* by *The Nosebleeds* was one of the early punk singles. I remember going to Manchester on the bus to buy it. It has a blisteringly brilliant guitar solo by Vini Reilly, later of Durutti Column.

the no-frills and I gravitated towards black and white ink drawings, wood engraving and woodblock prints.

Simon moved on from his *Theatre Fellow* job to work in Keswick at *The Century Theatre*. He organised a wonderful gig for Notsensibles at *The Braithwaite Institute*. It was there that I met his friend Chris Holden. Chris was an oriental arts dealer. He too was an old hippy and had even done the *Morocco Trail* back in the day. He was tall and thin with big bushy hair. He lived at *Greta Bank* in a wonderful farmhouse at the foot of Latrigg mountain. Chris was the one who got me more interested in Japanese prints – in particular the later printmaker *Ohara Koson*. Koson drew exquisitely from nature: birds; animals; fish.

Japanese printmaking is amazing. Each colour is printed separately using a different block. The ink is carefully wiped from the blocks to create shade or shadow. Some parts aren't inked at all but are embossed, again creating the impression of subtle shading and shadowing. People who don't know what they are think that they are water colours. Japanese prints have the signature of the author in black and a red stamp from the print studio. Because Koson was a later print maker (1877 – 1945), his prints used to be relatively common and cheap to collect. The more garish earlier Japanese prints of the Kabuki theatre are far more collectable. The Kabuki actors were the equivalent of film stars.

Chris and I became lifelong friends and I used to visit him regularly. Every time I went, I would stop off in Lancaster and go busking – it was a great busking town and I did well there. There used to be a great junk/antiques shop called *Vicary*. I would always go in and look for Japanese prints. I found a few Kosons there.

A couple of years before I met Chris, Inger and I went camping in the lakes. We were driving around the back roads North of Keswick when we came round a corner and chanced upon the most amazing purple wooden house. A PURPLE house. Right in the middle of the lake district!

Simon originally lived in a basement flat on Helvellyn St when he first moved to Keswick. A year or so later, he moved to a wacky house in the Newlands valley. All the local Bohos rented rooms there.

My friend Tom Winstanley and I drove up to visit him one day in my Morris Minor van. Tom was one of a bunch of new friends from Rossendale who I got to know after Notsensibles split. He was thin and languid and had the most outrageous politically incorrect sense of humour I've ever come across. He played drums in a covers band with a bunch of older blokes who were teachers. They were called *Victor Drago*. We became good friends and started playing music together. We had a two-piece band long before it was fashionable.

To find Simon's place we headed out of Keswick following his directions. We turned off the A66, along narrow meandering climbing roads and as we rounded a corner there it was – that same purple house. Simon had a little self-contained flat in a big ground floor room with a bay window and magnificent view. He'd just bought himself one of the first *Tascam Portastudios* and he had a neat little home recording set-up. Tom got a cold and when he was recovering, he wrote a song called *I feel better now* and recorded it on the Portastudio. There were a couple of rooms for rent and we seriously considered moving there but never did.

The house was owned by *Varya Vergauwen*. It was called *Rigg Beck*. She was originally from Switzerland and had moved to the lakes with her husband after studying at Westminster Art College. She bought it for £500 from a retired Major. The house had been built as a hotel and was a magnet for arty and theatrical types. Lots of famous people had stayed there. She was a wonderful eccentric jolly character and had a visitors book filled with interesting names including Peter Sellers.

One day, when she, Chris, Simon and I were talking about print-making, she pointed out a large heavy iron press on the landing windowsill. It had a big handle and a coarse thread that screwed down a heavy metal plate. It was ornate and obviously quite old. I thought it was a cider press or something similar. 'No, It's a nipping press.' She explained that nipping presses were used in bookbinding for clamping the finished book together. 'You can have it if you like.' Later I did a bit of research on bookbinding and started making sketch books and selling them. I still use the nipping press.

One day, I spotted a pair of Koson prints in a second-hand shop just up the road from our house. I was very excited. The shop was shut and there was a sign on the door saying 'back in five minutes.' Peering through the window, I spotted them on the back wall. I didn't need to be able to see the signature to recognise them instantly. The owner actually took half an hour to return during which time I'd already been back twice. I browsed round the shop and pretended to nonchalantly notice the prints.

'What are those?'
'They're Chinese silk paintings.'
'Oh. How much are they?'
'Thirty five.' (staged pause),
'OK – I'll have them.'

One of them is an exquisite scene of a crow on a flowering magnolia branch which remains one of my favourite Koson print ever.

Until fairly recently everything was printed using letterpress. Lead type was expertly clamped together to form text. Printing was a highly skilled artistic job. Spider had an *Adana* letterpress printing set-up that he used to print all the tickets for the Railway Workers and other local punk gigs. Adanas were fairly common. They are a small hand printing press that hobby printers and small businesses used. With the advent of easier ways of printing, they became obsolete. Not quite though. You can still get spares. I remember being inspired when I read about how the Bloomsbury set hand-printed their booklets.

I'm a bit of a typography nerd. Typography is about the meticulous arrangement of text on a page. The digital age has all but killed it off as an art form. I have some lovely old books on the subject[*]. Many years ago my uncle Jim in London had a printing business that he ran from his garden shed. He had a lithography printing machine supplemented by an Adana letter press setup and an A3 guillotine. I bought the lot from him for £100 and my brother and I drove down in The Chumbas' transit van to pick it up.

---

[*] Printing for Pleasure – John Ryder (Bodley Head – 1955). Introduction to Typography – Oliver Simon (Pelican – 1945). First Principles of Typography – Stanley Morrison (Cambridge University Press – 1936).

I sold the lithography press and I've since picked up other letterpress bits and pieces. They're housed in a botched-together cabinet in this alcove to the left of the fireplace. It's waist height, (I have a tall stool to sit on). It's made from bits of wood found in skips. With the window next to it, the lighting is good so it's the best place in the room to write. When we moved to this house I was going to chuck it and build another. I kept it to remind me of a time when I was completely skint. DIY was survival. The cabinet houses seven trays of type, two trays of woodblocks, two Adana presses and various printing sundries. It's a little self-contained print shop. There's more in the cupboards above. The guillotine is in the cellar. I use it all to print sleeves and labels for the tinpot fledgling record label. The woodblocks are cut Japanese-style. There are at least two for every record cover. There's a little adapter to print the record labels and a jig for scouring, folding and cutting card sleeves. The record label logo is blind-embossed into the bottom corner of every release.

Traditionally letterpress leaves a very fine subtle impression on the paper. By contrast, using lots of ink and embossing the images as deeply as possible into the card produces an image unmistakably different from anything that can be produced digitally. Smudges, finger prints, roller marks are inevitable – the perfect ones are actually the most boring. It's all very arts and crafts. Letterpress printing is a wonderful art form which adds a nice dimension to making records. It's also one of the few mediums that can't be emulated by digital technology. The idea to marry music, writing, art and design morphed into my little back-room record label.

'Give me 26 lead soldiers and I will conquer the world.'

Who said that?

I've always had a fascination for language. One of my old text books has a glossary of Greek and Latin names at the back. Here are a few examples (L = Latin, Gr = Greek):

albicans L. becoming white
arachnoid Gr. *Arachne* spider, spider's web + *-oid* like
pterigoid Gr. *Pterigos* wing + *-oid* like
scaphoid Gr. *scaphe* a skiff, a small boat + *-oid* like
scrotum L. a bag

It's intriguing that the whole range of common human experience can be expressed through such a myriad of different languages. The discovery of printing revolutionised language – the printed word became much more widely available to more ordinary people. Manuscripts hand-written by monks were superseded by letterpress and woodblock printing.

I did French at O level and A level and even though I gloriously failed the A level, I developed a love of the language – in fact languages in general. I also did German O level (and failed that too). The German teacher was scary and made us learn an entire passage (which I remember in full to this day *'Es is eine wunderschöne sommertag, die sonne sheint aus eine volkenlosen himmel...'*).

On the day that I finished my engineering apprenticeship, I went down town and bought a tent and some camping equipment. My dad gave me a lift to the M6 and I began a three month hitch-hiking journey around France and back. I had desperate wanderlust. I just had to get away. I had a restless inquisitiveness – a longing to look for something different – something that didn't exist in the grey rainy north of England. I didn't want to work in a factory. I didn't want to be part of a structure that made the rich richer and the poor poorer. Even at the naïve age of twenty the bolshy streak that probably came in equal parts from my mum and dad was showing through. I was questioning everything and developing a healthy disregard for authority and all that was pre-prescribed. Nine-to-five, university, job, mortgage, etc, etc.

Ironically when Notsensibles were going, I was so timid that I hardly did anything outrageous or radical (although we got up to lots of childish schoolboyish pranks). I did drink but I certainly didn't touch drugs – I was far too scared. I suppose something of the punk anti-establishment ethic must have rubbed off.

I don't travel much now, but it was certainly a good thing back then. It's good to put distance between the pre-ordained rut of daily life and investigate other possibilities. My destination was a village near Perpignan where my friend Andrew and a bunch of itinerant friends were camping in a field. Andrew had been a regular at The Railway Workers and was a close friend of Spider's. He had a big blonde quiff and a rockabilly look reminiscent of Brian Setzer. I'd never hitch-hiked before. It was quite an experience. Times have changed and I certainly wouldn't do it in this day and age. I was armed with a Collins French dictionary and a French grammar. I fell in love with France and The French – their suave sophistication, their sensuality, their food, their varied countryside and damn it their attitude to sex.* I soaked up the experience –

---

* We're British, we don't talk about that kind of thing.

looking up every word on every billboard. By the time I came back, I'd got to grips with the basics and could get by pretty well. At my zenith, someone once asked me if I was Belgian when trying to place my accent. Now that was a complement.*

The French are proud of their country and culture and can sometimes come across as xenophobic – particularly towards English thickos who can't be arsed to make the effort. They are not afraid of speaking up for what is right and complaining (unlike the English who say 'sorry' at the drop of a hat). I can't remember how I kept in touch with Andrew because there were no mobile phones or internet – just phone boxes and letters. I hitch-hiked for three days, with hardly any sleep. I finally found myself walking along a deserted pitch-black *Route Nationale* about ten miles from my destination. I was really scared and every time a car came past, I hid in the ditch. After a couple of hours, I was getting very tired and fed up. I saw a pair of headlights approaching in the distance and this time I stopped and put my thumb out. The car stopped. It was a Citroen 2CV.

The driver and his girlfriend where hippyesque. They were very kind and after rolling a big fat spliff, they took me directly to my destination after I showed them my scrap of

---

* I was too much of a blond-haired tomato to pass off as looking French.

paper. They dropped me off in the village square as the first streaks of light were appearing in the clear summer sky. I slept on the bus shelter bench for an hour or so. Through snoozing eyes, I saw a man on a bicycle carrying baguettes in a basket on the front and wearing a black beret. I was definitely in France. I can't remember how I found Andrew but I did. We drank cheap wine (cheap wine is cheap in France) and I promptly passed out. The weather was hot hot hot and humid. I loved it. One evening there was a heavy thunderstorm and I joyously huddled in my brand new tent marvelling at its waterproofness. We ate apricots straight from the trees.

I had a little set of watercolours with me and as I travelled, I did lots of drawing and painting – little pastiches of life in France. I did a little painting in The Louvre. I found the people wandering round the gallery as interesting as the paintings and I painted a girl on a bench with the Mona Lisa in the background. The painting's real name is *La Gioconda* (or La Joconde in French). Gioconda was the surname of the woman in the painting. It roughly translates as *The Smiling One*. The girl on the bench was the smiling one.

I like the Latin languages. They're simpler and more skeletal than English. English is a real mongrel – a hybrid of old French, Italian, German and Norse. There's even a smattering of Sanskrit. It's the ultimate immigrants' language – complicated – full of quirks. Maybe that's why the literature is so great – Shakespeare to name but one. It's interesting how language delineates race. We don't say, 'I speak British.' The Welsh speak Welsh. The Scots speak Scottish Gallic. The Irish speak Irish Gaelic (the most exquisite of all tongues – surely the language of the elves?). Even the Americans speak English (albeit a bastard hybrid).

I hate the dumbing down of the English language. I once saw a sign outside a pub: 'wanted proffesional chef.' Ha. Even worse is the creeping Americanisation of English. I've noticed recently the alarming rise of 'Hey' as a greeting. Round here, you can say 'o-reight,' or 'reight,' or 'y'orright.' 'Hiya' is acceptable but even 'Hi' is a bit modern and posh. Of course there's the Lancashire dialect expression 'Hey up' (with a silent aitch). Otherwise you would only ever use 'Hey' (also with a silent aitch) as a prefix to something derogatory such as 'hey dickhead,' or 'hey twat.'

Later I tried to learn Spanish too; my sister in law lived in Seville for a couple of years and we went out to visit her. The problem was that even if I managed to start a conversation, the replies were too fast and guttural for me to understand.

The language during my engineering apprenticeship was vernacular to say the least and that has always stayed. Vernacularity remains the default at our house. For example the pragmatic nuttiness of *twat* and all its possible commutations* can't be conveyed using any other word. Where I come from, a *STOP BEING A CUNT* sticker is infinitely preferable to a letter to *The Guardian*.

Years later, after I'd been back to school and got a 'proper job' we would have weekly meetings at work. Ewan was one of my colleagues. He can talk the bollocks off a donkey and is immensely literate and knowledgeable. With his monumental intellect he would fire off rat-a-tat oblique volleys of wit leaving me in paroxysms of laughter, thus relieving the stultifying tedium of an otherwise unbearable experience.

At one meeting, after yet another onslaught from the management, I said, 'We few, we happy few, we band of brothers.' Ewan immediately got the reference. It's from King Henry's St Crispin's day speech in Shakespeare's Henry V. I'm not literary – I only know it because my dad used to regularly recite it. If I asked Ewan about a point of grammar he would type out a little sheet for me with examples. My favourite rant of his was the analogy of an out-of-hand students party where they're all spilling out onto the street. I can't quite remember what the analogy

---

* Twat, twat-face, twat-hat, twat-pants, twatness, twat-phone, twatting, twatted, twattification, twat-trum, twattify, detwattify and so on.

was – probably something to do with management and overcrowding. I just thought it sounded like a great party. If Ewan and I were in the same class at school, I think we would both be the naughty boys – he would be the loud one who got bullied by the teacher and made to stand at the front of the class. I would be the quieter shy one with a good idea where to place the cat in order to scatter the pigeons – there are definitely some Laurel and Hardy credentials there.

Speech has to be pretty important. The Buddhists nailed it with several lists which come under the heading of *right speech*. Maybe the use of the vernacular is fine if it's used in a non-malicious context?

Finally, there's the 'C' word – understandably deeply offensive to many – particularly girls and my American friends. It's not as bad as it used to be. My friends Ruth and Vicky, both staunch defenders of women as equals to men, and as down-to-earth as me, use it freely. It's taken on a certain chic in some lesbian circles and I've seen it used at least once on the front page of one of the posher daily newspapers.* I don't use it much. Sometimes though, no

---

* It was when a spoilt overpaid cunt of a footballer had called another spoilt-cunt overpaid footballer a cunt during a match. There ensued a long expensive Football Association investigation where several pompous snivelling football management cunts feigned outrage at the use of the word cunt on the pitch. Cunts.

other word will do. Why use twenty words when you can use one? Why use twenty letters when four suffice?

My sweetness can be the most cuttingly direct person in the world (and very artistic). We were once out somewhere when we were nauseatingly asked if we had pet names for each other. She was quicker than me. I don't know which came first – the searingly dry facial expression or the one-word answer. It happened in an instant. The question-asker was clearly taken aback.

Maybe art gives food to the soul? A bit of passion – fuel for the engine? Is the ranch art? Is there art on the ranch?

The wren's nest in the coat pocket; the exquisite contour of the yellow flag iris; the indescribable beauty of the patterned designs on the wings of the sparrowhawk; the concrete pair of bosoms on the ramp up from the gates at the top (it's my builder's joke). I keep meaning to do a bumprint, but haven't got round to it yet.

5. Don Juan, The Buddha and me.

Type cabinet, back room. Sun 14th December.

Winter has settled into its north-west England grey drizzly pall. Keeping on top of the ranch becomes more of a chore. Today it's been a bit grim. I've pruned a section of hedge. I had to light the stove in demi-shed B to get warm – my fingers were going numb. Coming home to the warm house and Sunday dinner is bliss. I refitted the kitchen a couple of years ago and now we have a wood-burner. It's gorgeous. It keeps the kitchen and my room warm. It's transformed our lives. The kitchen was freezing before that. When I knocked off the plaster, the original stone lintel was there, so we made a feature of it. There's loads of room either side of the stove for drying firewood.

Every autumn, I plant hawthorn berries in a mixture of soil and sand. I leave them somewhere shaded and they take eighteen months or so to germinate. Germination is variable. Some years I hardly get any seedlings and other years I get a lot. The seeds need a cold snap before they germinate – it's called stratification. You can cheat and put them in the fridge for a while.

The hedge is about 80% hawthorn which is the best hedging plant for this part of the country – tough and durable. Dog rose is great too. When pruning, I weave its long barbed branches in and out of the top of the hedge – natural barbed wire. Holly is superb for privacy but it's very slow growing. I've finally had some success from cuttings. Willow is wonderfully versatile. Every year, I make rough woven hurdles from its long straight supple branches and put them back into the hedge for added privacy. There are two large goat willow trees in the allotment above. In spring hundreds of their tiny floating seeds (like miniature dandelion seeds) take root in plant pots and borders. I replant them and bring them on for more hedging. They're supposed to be very good for bees. Blackthorn and hazel are great hedging plants too. If I ever get round to selling plants, native hedging will definitely feature.

A few years ago, I built a big plant stand that has a flat top with sides. I use it to cultivate various seedlings including trees. Underneath is a shelf that houses the majority of my plant pots. It's the perfect environment for snails to hibernate – they like to hang out around black plastic. In late winter, I clean the whole thing out and pick out a hundred or more of the blighters before they come out of hibernation. I put them in a bucket and walk to the top of the track and put them a dark corner. Apparently if you release them too close to where you find them, they just come back.

There didn't use to be so many snails. They've somehow taken over. They seem to be more intelligent and resourceful than slugs. In damp weather especially, they cause complete devastation of certain crops such as French beans. They even climb trees. I've got a system that is quite effective. In fact it could form the basis for an incisive essay or even a novelette:

Slugs and snails can't swim or fly – a mollusc treatise by Quentin Divington.

Crawling Slowly – The Mollusc Chronicles, by Sheenagh Gripplethorpe.

I never bought the idea of an omnipotent being other than the planet itself. If I had a religion, it would be nature: The annual cycle; the sun; the wind; the plants; birth; life; death; the animals – including human beings. Nature is at the heart of most religions. The further I am from nature, the more miserable I become. How did all this mysterious magnificent system come about? The geometry, the symmetry of certain plants and animals? The sublime architecture? The resilience? The variety? Utterly magical.

My dad used to make us go to church. As soon as I had a choice, I never went again. I did like the poetry of the King James bible though*. I like a lot of its nuggets of universal wisdom that transcend all religions.

And why take ye thought for raiment? Consider the lilies of the field, how they grow. They toil not, neither do they spin, and yet I say unto you that even Solomon in all his glory was not arrayed like one of these.

And again I say unto you, it is easier for a camel to go through the eye of a needle, than for a rich man to enter into the kingdom of God.

As ye sow, so shall ye reap.

I understand why human beings need religion. People need some kind of guidance and structure. A lot of the ancient cultivation methods of tribal societies are interwoven with their spiritual beliefs.

As children, my brother and I were a few years behind everyone else when it came to getting the latest gadgets.

'Please can we have a telly? Everyone else has one.'
'Er – the starving children of Africa don't have tellies.'

---

* Until some dicks destroyed it by doing patronising banal up-to-date interpretations.

One of the first things I remember watching when we finally did get one was *Kung Fu* starring David Carradine. I loved it. It was a 'goody wins in the end' American wild West type series but the goody was an exiled Shaolin monk. The highlights were the flashbacks to the Shaolin temple and the little nuggets of Buddhist wisdom. Back in the days of Notsensibles, Simon introduced Inger and me to the *I Ching*. He would flamboyantly throw it open and say, 'Read any page, man – It's all gold!'

Via Simon and Chris and other friends, I started getting more into Eastern philosophy and reading lots of books: *The way of Zen* by Alan Watts. *Zen Flesh, Zen Bones* by Paul Reps. *Zen in The Art of Archery* by Eugene Herrigel and so on. Sheila and James, our lovely friends from Bacup, had moved to Liverpool and we used to visit them there. They introduced me to Carlos Castaneda. One day Sheila, wise and demure with long auburn hair, handed me a book.

'You might like this.'

It was *The Teachings of Don Juan*. Castaneda was a student of anthropology at the University of California, Los Angeles

---

* The I Ching is an ancient book of Chinese divination from the Taoist and Confucian traditions. It was translated into German by Richard Wilhelm and later into English (first published in the UK in 1951).

during the mid sixties. He purportedly met a Yaqui Indian named Juan Matus whilst on a field trip to Mexico. He was looking for someone to teach him about the medicinal properties of the plants local to the area. That kind of thing is right up my street, so the book grabbed my attention. Don Juan subsequently took Castaneda on as an apprentice in an ancient system of Indian shamanism and knowledge. I read the book but didn't think much of it. There are accounts of divination carried out using *Datura* and lizards. It all sounded a bit hippy-dippy to me. What did grab me though was a passage written in Spanish at the beginning of the introduction. The English translation was underneath. There was something about it that appealed enormously to me.

For me there is only the travelling on paths that have heart,
on any path that may have heart. There I travel, and the only
worth-while challenge is to traverse its full length.
And there I travel looking, looking breathlessly.

Follow the path with a heart. I like that. That will do for me.

I went on to read his subsequent books: *A separate Reality, Journey to Ixtlan and Tales of Power*. I found these books a lot more engaging and hugely inspiring. They move away from hallucogenics and recount Castaneda's pragmatic encounters with a mysterious and inscrutable old Indian.

There are countless long hikes in the desert and Mexican countryside where Carlos is constantly confounded by Don Juan's physical and intellectual knowledge and prowess. Some of the accounts defy the imagination but underlying it all is the story of native people who can live off the land with imaginative aplomb. Their knowledge of local plants was unsurpassed. It's not quite allotmenteering, but there's a common theme – you can't beat a bit of romance and mystery.

Don Juan constantly challenges Carlos's preconceptions. His teachings are based on aspiring to behave 'as a warrior'. It's nothing whatsoever to do with fighting or violence. It's about a code of conduct – a concise way of living that frees up the energy to become a 'man of knowledge'. Don Juan uses 'man of knowledge' in the context of himself and his fellow sorcerers but there are equally formidable female sorcerers in the stories.

In Journey to Ixtlan he introduces a number of pragmatic themes such as 'Taking responsibility', 'Death as an advisor', 'Disrupting the routines of daily life', 'A worthy opponent' and 'Erasing personal history'.

He teaches the concept of 'stalking' as not only a way of hunting, but also as a way of achieving pragmatic goals in everyday life and personal development. He uses wonderful poetic metaphors such as 'cubic centimetre of chance', 'controlled folly', and 'having to believe'. Journey To Ixtlan in particular had an enormous influence on me and I've read it loads of times. After the first four books, Castaneda continued writing about his relationship with Don Juan. His later books become increasingly convoluted and weird. People speculate that these were just a money-making exercise and they were probably written after Don Juan's death. I have no doubt that Don Juan did exist. The extent to which Castaneda embellished the character will probably never be known.

Around the time I was reading Don Juan, I was looking around for a kung-fu or T'ai Chi class but there were none locally. Tom had started going to a Buddhist meditation class. I was trying to get my head together and free myself from my shitty moods. From the influence of people like Simon and Chris, It was only natural that I gravitated towards Eastern philosophy.

'You should come, it's great.'

I did go and give it a try but I didn't like it. It wasn't my cup of tea. Everyone in the class sat down, then the teacher crept in silently and started speaking in a whisper. I remember thinking, 'Speak up mate.'

I don't know quite why I went back the week after. I found the whole thing rather nimby-pimby and irritating.

I'm not into any kind of religious ritual so the bowing in front of a statue aspect just didn't appeal to me one bit. What did appeal though was the 'Find out for yourself and make up your own mind.'

About fifteen years later I was still doing the meditation. On a cold November Friday, I went to the national centre for a weekend. (A beautiful farm in Wales). I explained to the meditation teacher that I was a fraud because I'd never accepted any of the religious aspects of Buddhism. He smiled and asked me how many people from the original group from all those years ago were still going to the class. Hmm. That would be just me. Maybe there's something in it?

Another time, I was talking to my meditation teacher about livelihood (right livelihood is a big theme in Buddhism). I was a busker at the time and making an OK living, but I was bored and looking for something else. He said that sometimes the very last thing that we expected was the right thing for us. That turned out to be quite prophetic.

Meditation somehow works on a subconscious level – quite how, I don't know. It's an oil that invisibly lubricates the wheels and guides you in the right direction. If you can get through the initial stages of learning the practice (a large percentage drop out), it becomes a beneficial part of daily life. You could say that it somehow links mind and body, providing useful exercise for the mind. It also allows a glimpse of something that the hippies might call 'universal love'. It's particularly useful before a task such as going to work or a recording session. It gives you more energy too and you need less sleep. It teaches that everything we need is already there – it's just a question of washing away the dust in order to be able to see it – ditching ballast so the balloon can clear the hilltop.

Even now, I've never accepted the religious aspects of Buddhism but I'm a bit of a list person on the quiet and Buddhism is full of lists*. The thing I like about it, is its provision of a map for the endlessly complicated slippery human mind. I also like the wonderful use of poetic analogies and stories.

A central part of meditation is the development of mind-fulness – it's about being aware in the present moment. Recently mindfulness has become trendy and it's actually quite alarming. It's a typical western yuppy phenomenon of taking an isolated aspect from an ancient system and using it as some kind of social sticking plaster.

---

* The four Noble Truths; The five precepts; The seven enlightenment factors; The twelve parts of dependent origination; The ten perfections – there are lots.

The one essential thing about meditation is to have an experienced teacher. 'The eye cannot see itself.' The modern phenomenon can actually be dangerous. And as for a 'mindfulness phone app' – utter bollocks. Buddhism is also filled with references to plants and nature – again, right up allotment street.

Coincidentally, after a few years of doing the meditation, the teacher said that I needed to do something energetic. He suggested morris dancing or kung fu. Guess which one I chose?

6. Busker

2nd February. Type cabinet, back room.

My sense of reality is often grievously impaired by a myriad of romantic illusions, some of them too ridiculous to mention. There are times when I have raised buffoonery to the highest of art forms.

Why shouldn't I be a bohemian Leonardoesque eccentric? I shall drive around in an old VW split-screen van. I will have a one-acre smallholding and grow most of my own food. Where's my tractor? I'll make records and daft music videos. I'll write books and go on tour. I'll have an inquisitive interest in science. I might even study medicine. Oh well – if you don't believe in your dreams and strive for them, they'll never happen.

I've always been a believer in the hunter-gatherer philosophy – take what you need and no more and leave the environment as you found it (or better still, improve it). It's a model that works on a myriad of levels, admirably applicable to allotmenteering – developing a sustainable garden that provides most of your food for years to come. What a wonderful idea.

There are the days on the ranch when I find the place overwhelming. Scrabbling around on a scruffy weed patch for the sake of a few potatoes and blackcurrants. Enduring a penetrating pall of grey rain and squelching and sliding on the slimy slippery paths. There's always so much to do. What's the point? That's the nature of doubt. Its dark clinging tentacles creep in and insidiously soften the edges of good intentions and lofty aspirations.

Today I've had a dreary couple of hours up there in the clinging drizzle, weeding and tidying. Still, it's good to get outside rain or shine. I should have realised early on that I wasn't cut out for the indoor nine-to-five life.

My contemplative hitch-hiking trip to France all those years ago was the first step towards looking at other ways to make a living. In the hot sultry south, life was slow and sedate. We lived off baguettes, Camembert, tomatoes and olives and the cheapest wine that the French reserved for cooking only.

After I'd met up with Andrew, we'd stayed a week or so in the field where he was camping before heading off to the beach to a hippy/anarchist commune. My abiding memory is of lots of gorgeous women walking around naked. The sea was warm and the weather was baking hot. Our plan was to head north to Bordeaux where we had friends. Chris and Annette, guitarist and sax player from *The Stuffed Badgers* had moved there a year or so previously. The Stuffed Badgers were one of the many bands who sprang up locally at the time of punk. Under the auspices of his *Theatre Fellow* job at the arts association, Simon had started a musicians' collective and a healthy music scene developed.

Chris and Annette lived in a fourth floor one-bedroom flat in a fairly central area. Along with their friend Didier, they made a living out of busking. Bordeaux is a lovely city. There's a long charming pedestrianised thoroughfare and tall multi-storeyed tenements lining the streets.

In the South of France, everything shuts down in the hot midday then opens again in the late afternoon and early evening. The best time for busking was when the shops reopened. Andrew and I would go with Chris and Annette and Didier and watch them play. They also did gigs in bars. It was hard work but they were making a living out of it. The other buskers who stuck in my memory were a banjo player and a soprano saxophonist. They were phenomenally good and clearly were making a lot of money.

I didn't really want to go back to a 'proper job'. I wanted to do something independent. Something artistic. Maybe I could have a go at busking? No way was I going to strum and sing but I had a budding interest in classical guitar – maybe I could learn some solo guitar pieces and do that?

A few days after we arrived in Bordeaux, Chris and Annette headed back to England for a break and left us to look after their flat. Andrew and I didn't have much money, but we had a great time wandering the magical atmospheric streets of Bordeaux.

Directly opposite on the other side of the street lived a French couple with two little girls. They waved at us regularly and one day they invited us across. They were very hospitable and charming and we became friends. They were called Ann and Didier (another Didier). They also made their living on the streets. They made and sold jewellery from a small portable stall.

After a week or so, Andrew went back to England and I had the flat to myself. I spent most of my time with Ann and Didier. They rented a small farm cottage in the countryside an hour's drive from Bordeaux. They invited me with them for a weekend and we had a wonderful time. They drove a lovely old dark blue *Citroen 103*. We went to a nudist beach and in the evening we went to a club where the DJ played great R&B and funk.

By the time I got home, I knew what I wanted to do. Music of course and to start with, I was going to be a busker. I sat down and spent hour upon hour learning a handful of solo guitar pieces. I had a red Epiphone semi-acoustic guitar and I bought a small Vox amp powered by a six-volt battery.

The moment of truth came and I walked down town and set up in the walk-way from the market square. I was shaking so much that I could hardly play. I persevered and seemed to do pretty well. I can't remember how long I played. I walked home in feverish excitement. I was still living with my mum and dad. I emptied the change onto the kitchen table and to my amazement I'd made sixty four quid and thirty six pence. It was a eureka moment. Here was something I could do for myself and hopefully make enough money to live off.

For the next five years, that's exactly what I did. I slowly built up a large repertoire of classical and finger-picking pieces. I travelled to every town within thirty miles (I never busked in my home town again). I was always careful not to outstay my welcome. I'd play for a couple of hours then move on, hoping not to annoy shopkeepers.

The Vox was expensive on batteries so I built my own little busking amp. It was based around a ten-inch speaker, a motorbike battery and a cheap amplifier kit from *Maplin*.

I had no electronics knowledge. My friend Andy soldered it up for me then I made the cab around the parts.

The speaker was angled slightly upwards. The top hinged up to access the battery. The amp doubled as a seat and I upholstered the lid. I made a rucksack to carry it. The front unzipped and rolled up so I could just take off the rucksack, put it on the floor, unzip the front and I was off. It's still in the attic somewhere. I had a Morris Minor van at the time. I found the best routes to all the towns and parking spots on the outskirts where I didn't have to pay.

One day I was busking in the centre of Bradford and a bloke stopped and watched me for several minutes. He came and talked to me. He was very polite and encouraging and carried a quiet gentle authority. He clearly was very knowledgeable about music. I was still playing my Epiphone. He suggested that my pieces would sound much better played on a classical guitar. In the most skilful and diplomatic of ways he suggested that because of the technical skills involved, I might benefit from some guitar lessons. I didn't need lessons. I could teach myself anything. I belong to the *I ain't been to no music school* school of music – remember?

My youthful self-determination inevitably carried a certain amount of arrogance. Still, there was something very engaging and authoritative about him. With hindsight, I suspect that he was probably a music teacher of the highest order. He certainly gave me a powerful lesson.

It wasn't long before I walked into a music shop and traded the Epi for a Yamaha classical fitted with a transducer pickup. The Epi was probably worth at least three times more than the Yamaha and today it would be worth more than ten times – It was a *Kalamazoo*-built model. That wasn't the point. It was my living and I needed a guitar straight away.

I found a guitar teacher and had lessons for a year or two. I did up to grade 6 classical guitar and grade 5 theory of music. I was incredibly nervous during the exams. The bloke in Bradford was right. The lessons stood me in good stead.

When I wasn't out busking, I practised several hours a day. At my peak I had a vast repertoire of pieces and I was attempting a few concert pieces (Requerdos de la Alhambra, Leyanda, Prelude in D). I always played from memory. I was making a decent living and was getting asked to play concerts and in restaurants.

I don't consider myself musical in any way. Some people can just listen to a song and play it. I have to get hold of the music and learn it by rote – painful note by painful note. I did learn a couple of pieces by listening to the recording because there was no sheet music available. The wonderful *Fisherman's Lilt* played by Dan Ar Bras is one example.

It was an interesting period. I played guitar several hours a day and at one point I started to get back problems. I sorted it out by reading about *The Alexander Technique*. During this time I moved out of my mum and dad's house and lived a very frugal disciplined life. I got rid of a lot of my possessions and painted everything in the house white.

I used to produce a fanzine and I organised an art exhibition. I met a girl wearing a tatty leopard-skin top. She wanted to be in the exhibition. She made two alien-like pink life-size figures clasping forks and knives. She used to come with me when I went busking. She got to scour every shopping centre within a thirty mile radius. Ah – the posh charity shops of Harrogate. It must have been tough.

At the time, my rented house was missing a back gate. Coincidentally, one day, I spotted a figure in the distance, bent double, carrying a door. It was her. She's very practical like that. She has a magpie eye for large improbable objects – fireplaces, lumps of stone. You name it, she's found it. Whereas I'm a hunter-gatherer, she's more of a gatherer. I sometimes call her *The Finder*. When any of us lose stuff in the house, she will always find it. She's also very comical. Her coruscating no-bullshit down-to-earth insightfulness often has us in paroxysms of laughter. In a loud whisper she will often come out with phrases such as, 'Christ, look at the size of her arse!' and, 'I don't like him – he's got a pinhead.' I will say, 'Ah, I see you're rehearsing for *the tactlessness of the century award* again. She's fascinated with good hair[*] and I jokingly pretend that she's written a book called *Heads and Hair*. Whenever I catch her staring at a fine mop I say 'Does that get a page in the book?' She reminds me of a charming animal that snuffles about and hides things in secret corners. Her directness translates into the most wonderful and unusual eye for all things art and fashion. She's forever picking up interesting clothes from charity shops and she makes extra-ordinary jewellery from things like plastic crocodiles. In fact she's just bought a fluorescent green ice cube tray which she's going to cut up and make into a necklace – the spaces for the ice cubes are arrow-shaped. I keep saying to her that she should open a shop but she always replies that she would never be able to get rid of anything. Her Aladdin's cave is certainly a testament to that.

My songwriting was prolific in those days and Tom and I were doing regular gigs. After one gig, someone made a comment about the last song. 'That's the best love song I've ever heard.' When I later recorded the song, I found a

---

[*] I used to have thick blonde wavy hair. I wouldn't have stood a chance otherwise.

trumpet player because I knew the girl liked trumpet. He was called Alex Shields and I spotted him playing in a band called *Whipping Post*. I went to his mum's house in Shipley to rehearse it then we recorded it at the recording studio at Nelson and Colne College. My brother played drums and Nash played bass. My film-maker friend Tom Bruggen used a clip of the song in one of his films.

I had a period of going to gigs with my friend and accomplished folk singer Kath Reade. I'd play guitar with her then play a few solo guitar pieces. It was good fun. She sang backing vocals on the recording. Alex and Kath are also on *Under The Archway* – a twee little song that I wrote about the ranch.

The biggest hindrance when busking was other buskers. The worst were rude fuckers who set up close by and drowned me out. During this period my musical snobbery became even more honed. I never liked bland guitar strumming and I never will. My worst imaginable gig is having to listen to droves of fucking strummers before it's my turn to play. I don't do those kinds of gigs any more. I honestly can't bear to hear Dylan's *Blowing in The Wind* ever again.

Hence the hunting ethic – learning which spot to head for – exactly when and where and how to avoid other buskers. I was an early bird. I would beat the rush. I went back to

Bordeaux and busked there (carrying a guitar and amp and all my camping gear was no joke). I also busked my way through Spain.

One day I was busking outside M&S in one of the myriad northern towns beginning with 'B'. A bloke approached me and asked me if I fancied coming and playing at a gig that he was organising.

Tom and I had our two-piece at the time. We both wrote songs and sang. I used a splitter to feed into two guitar amps – one each side of the drum kit. One amp was set to be very bassy and the other had a clean guitar sound that could be over-driven with my distortion pedal. Tom was a great drummer and at full pelt we were stonkingly loud and powerful. We also had lots of quieter songs. Tom cleverly played drums and keyboard at the same time on some songs. He had a very pragmatic way of keeping things going with string and tape. I called it 'Tom Tech'. Two-pieces are very fashionable now, especially with the advent of fancy foot pedals. We were the only one around at the time. We were like *The White Stripes* but better. I said to the bloke that I'd rather play with my band and he said that was fine.

The bloke was Fenny and that was the start of a lifelong friendship. Busking gave me a few adventures, improved my guitar playing and made me a living for five years. In the end though, I got fed up of it. It was a lonely life and a new chapter beckoned. The girl who carried the back door and I eventually moved in together. Next thing, we had a baby girl and it was time to do something else.

7. Emergency

Sat 21st March. Type cabinet, back room.

Spring is here. The days are getting longer and the evenings will be light again. Bright green hawthorn leaves are appearing in the hedge and the daffodils are out. I've been up since six. I was on the ranch by half past. It's bursting with life. I stand at the top and survey the view. The crisp air and cool blue sky are stunning. Birds are singing and I catch a glimpse of the sparrowhawk swooping low over the hedge. I've shifted the horse shit, planted loads of seeds and done a bit of bottle building. I can't think of anywhere I'd rather be. I could happily work up here all day every day. Unfortunately I have to go to *work* later but at least I've had a couple of hours outdoors.

Into the fray and it's 12:45. We get a standby call for a 47 year old man in cardiac arrest. All emergency departments have standby phones in their resuscitation rooms to take calls directly from ambulance crews who are bringing in an emergency. The man has had bystander CPR and has been shocked twice with a defibrillator. He's still in VF and they're six minutes away. VF means ventricular fibrillation whereby the main chambers of the heart are quivering uncontrollably rather than pumping as they should. It's fatal if not converted back to a normal rhythm using an electric shock from a defibrillator.

We prepare bay 2 in the resusc room. There's me, my favourite resusc nurse, a Senior House Officer (SHO), a student nurse and a Healthcare Assistant (HCA). I get out two cannulas and all the blood bottles.

The ambulance arrives and we get the patient across onto the hospital trolley as the crew hand over. Apparently he was in a café reading a newspaper and complained of chest pain then staggered outside and collapsed. A passer-by started CPR pretty quickly. We don't know anything else about him.

He's not intubated and has one green cannula in the back of his right hand. The paramedic carries on delivering oxygen to the patient using a bag and mask. We get the defibrillator leads on and he's still in VF so we shock him. The student nurse takes over CPR and the SHO puts in another cannula and takes bloods. There's a very well-established routine for treating cardiac arrest in the UK which is overseen by *The Resuscitation Council of England.*

His last adrenaline was over three minutes ago. One milligram of adrenaline is given every three to five minutes. My favourite resusc nurse silently hands me another without any prompting and as I think about Amiodarone she's already got it out and handed it to me – the drug is typically given after three unsuccessful shocks. It's used to treat many different kinds of abnormal heart rhythm.

After two minutes, we pause to check the rhythm – he's still in VF so we shock again and carry on. He looks to be in his mid forties.

I get the laryngoscopes out of the top drawer – a 3 and a 4 blade and a size 8 tube and a bougie just in case. I put the suction under the mattress and hook up a Water's circuit with a filter and a CO_2 probe. All these things are pieces of equipment used to carry out intubation, which involves visualizing the patient's vocal cords and passing a tube between them. The laryngoscope is a torch with a handle and a curved blade that lifts the tongue to one side allowing the vocal cords to be seen.

His teeth look to be in good nick and his chin isn't big. These are factors that give you an idea of how easy or difficult an intubation might be. The next pulse check comes and after a bit of suctioning, I get a good view of his cords and tube him without difficulty. He's no longer in VF – he's in a very odd looking rhythm with a rate of about 50. We can't feel a pulse so we carry on CPR.

I ask for the ultrasound machine and I put the cardiac probe on his chest. I see that the main chambers of the heart, the ventricles, are both pumping, but the left ventricle – the one that does the most work is a bit floppy and lagging behind. This strongly suggests a heart attack (routinely referred to as an MI or myocardial infarction). At the next pulse check, there is a pulse and it's fairly strong – it's too early to tell whether it's adrenaline-dependent.

His heart rate is now 60 and we get an initial BP reading of 62/40. We give him cautious fluids (we don't want to overload his heart) and hook up the ventilator. I give a bit of Metaraminol which effectively constricts the peripheral blood vessels, leading to a rise in blood pressure. His BP rapidly improves to 124/72 which means that he's now getting a reasonable blood supply to his vital organs.

He starts to gag on his tube meaning that he's waking up so we start propofol and give him a small dose of fentanyl and some rocuronium. At this stage, it's safer to keep him intubated and anaesthetised. I phone the anaesthetist and put in an arterial line which allows continual measurement of the blood pressure using a transducer. We start cooling the patient with ice in plastic bags under his armpits and pillow cases and cold bags of saline out of the fridge. There's reasonable evidence that cooling a patient after a cardiac arrest improves their chance of survival. It's something to do with reducing the metabolic rate and therefore the oxygen demand.

The ECG shows an atypical ischaemic regular rhythm. ECG stands for electrocardiogram. It interprets the electrical activity of the heart onto a graph. Ischaemia means reduced blood supply. Most of these medical terms come from Latin and Greek. It's highly likely that he's had an MI.

The next crucial step is to arrange PCI and stenting to try and save his myocardium. Until relatively recently, heart attacks were treated with a clot-busting drug but this has been superseded by passing a fine catheter either through the radial artery or femoral artery and threading it all the way to the heart. Radio-opaque dye is then pumped through the catheter and the coronary arteries are visualized with an x-ray machine. Once the blockage is found, a balloon is carefully inflated to try and unblock it then a minute compressed stent is passed over the catheter and released across the blockage where it expands to keep the artery open. The technology and skill involved is astounding. The whole process is referred to as 'PCI' meaning *Percutaneous Coronary Intervention*. Myocardium is heart muscle. PCI takes place in a very specialised room known as a 'cath lab' (catheter laboratory). Ambulance crews are trained to recognise heart attacks on an ECG and take the patient directly to the nearest specialist hospital that has a cath lab. Likewise, if a patient develops a heart attack in a district general hospital, there's a slick process for referring and transferring them quickly to a specialist centre. Hospitals that have specialist services such as PCI, neurosurgery, trauma and cardiothoracic surgery are known as tertiary centres. Hospital medicine is broadly referred to as 'secondary care' and general practice and other community healthcare services are referred to as 'primary care'.

It just so happens that we have our own catheter lab downstairs. We were developing an excellent service but due to the ongoing development of a regional network, we are supposed to transfer the patient to a nearby hospital which has just been designated as the tertiary centre – it's all a bit contentious. I ring down anyway on spec and my mate Rani is there. 'Just give him 180 of Ticagrelor and get him straight down.' Ticagrelor is an anti-platelet drug that effectively makes the blood less sticky and less likely to clot during PCI. The anaesthetist arrives and ten minutes later the patient is out of the department and on his way to the cath lab. Rani phones back later to say that he successfully stented the patient's LAD and that the echo showed an ejection fraction of 60% which is good news. The LAD is the *Left Anterior Descending* coronary artery which supplies the left ventricle. Echo is short for echocardiogram which is basically an ultrasound of the heart. Some A&E doctors have a rudimentary grasp of echocardiography but cardiologists are highly trained and they can visualise the heart chambers and valves in great detail. The ejection fraction is a measure of how effectively blood is being pumped from the left ventricle. The day after, the patient is extubated and moved to coronary care. I pop in and see him. He's a fit active chap and we expect him to make a good recovery. He's very grateful.

Survival from out-of-hospital cardiac arrest is pretty rare. People say that when your time's up your time's up but I like to think that occasionally when people get to us in time there's a chance of saving them from the jaws of death for a bit longer. I always remember that cheesy proverb at the end of the titles of one of Spielberg's films: *Whosoever saveth a life saveth life entire.*

Back in the department, I'm chatting to Zina, one of the sisters. I've worked with her since day one and she knows me well. She has a very deadpan approach whenever I start snivelling. She often says things like, 'Oh Stephen, when will you learn?' and, 'Just accept that you're meant to be here.' She's laughing because I'm telling her that our dog had got an upset stomach this morning and had shat on the floor of my room. In our house, next to the kitchen (where I'm writing) is my multi-purpose room. In it I write, make things, record, rehearse, print, play records and so on. It's also a comfortable sitting room with an open fire. I've made a big desk and lots of shelving for records. My brother built cupboards above the doors right up to the high ceiling. He made a folding ladder to get up to them. I try and make the absolute most of the space. I jokingly call it my gentleman's chambers. I tell Zina that I'm writing a book and she says, 'Ooh am I in it?' She finds it inconsolably hilarious that a dog has shat in Doctor Hartley's chambers.

There's a lot of unspoken unconditional love in A&E between those in it for the long haul. There's also a certain kind of humility that's hard to explain. Nurses and doctors (and everyone else who works there) are just ordinary decent people yet they have a certain acceptance of all shades of humanity that you don't quite see anywhere else.

No telly programme could ever convey what A&E is really like. My favourite ever was *Green Wing* that somehow managed to convey a bit of the black humour and the surreal side of it. Those-fly-on-the wall documentaries irritate me because they're heavily edited and tend to romanticise the reality. Most of all I dislike those programmes with smarmy 'celebrity' doctors talking about people's distressing medical problems. Maybe I'm old-fashioned but I think it's just plain wrong. Patient confidentiality is enshrined in medical practice for a very good reason. Anyone with any illness is in a vulnerable position. Broadcasting it to millions, despite what anyone says, is a breach of confidentiality. The patients who agree to it obviously give their consent but if they're living with a distressing condition, are they really able to give consent in a balanced way? I don't watch medical programmes any more.

I'm a bit of a hypocrite because I simply don't believe in a lot of western medicine. We have an astounding immune system of mind-boggling complexity that has developed over millions of years and then we bugger it up with anti-biotics and drugs of questionable efficacy.

Kids need to get snuffles and infections to build up their herd immunity. Giving them antibiotics unnecessarily at the most delicate stage of their development in my opinion is a serious crime. Once again I'm in the minority-of-one club. What has caused the astonishing rise in the incidence of cancer over a relatively short period of time? I think it's partly due to the chronic poisoning of the food chain and partly due to the indiscriminate shelling out of antibiotics, particularly in early life. My conviction is observational and intuitive with no 'scientific' evidence base, so it counts for nothing.

I can't help smiling at the emergence of smug lifestyle books written by doctors. I could write such a book; the trouble is there would be no market for it because it would only be six sentences long: Eat and drink well; get outside; exercise well; be very careful which drugs you take; form good relationships with other living things; strive to learn and use time efficiently. Then there's mental health – such a big topic. I think a large percentage of it is down to loneliness and the fracturing of ordinary decent human society where everyone should have a place and look after each other.

Dr Fartley's casebook – a lifestyle guide from The Twat of The North.

I once was a busker then I became an A&E consultant. Now that's an unlikely tale.

8. Wheels

Thurs 14th May. 9.30 pm
Table, top of ranch.

'The darling buds of May'.

May is my favourite month. Spring hurtles towards summer. Joy of joy I'm off work and I've been up here since 7.30 doing my little morning routine: exercise; meditation; writing; breakfast. May has been pretty wet and rainy so far. Now it's delivered and we have a hot sunny spell. The plants are ecstatic. Everything is growing so fast, including the weeds. The sky is crystal blue and there's a light breeze. It's already hot. Today I'll be pottering with plants. I wait until mid-May to be safe from frost. There are loads of runner beans to go out. They're tough and well hardened off in big pots, but they are the snails' favourites and there will be a battle. The first week is crucial. I don't kill anything but I do use beer traps.

Slugs and snails love beer but then so do I so I don't waste money. I just use sugar, water and yeast and it works fine. I use the cut-off tops of plastic bottles. Where you put them makes a big difference. Hiding them under the edge of an already established plant seems to yield a much bigger haul. I simply put a spoonful of sugar in the bottom of the trap, then I activate the yeast in warm water. The icing on the cake is the addition of a small dog biscuit.

We once left the dog's bowl outside and there were a few biscuits left in it. When I went out into the yard fairly late on, I observed several slugs in the bowl chewing on the biscuits.

I'm seated at my writing table in its usual position, overseeing the best view. To my right in the top corner of the ranch, is an elder tree. I planted it from a ten-inch cutting years ago and it took root. Now it's fifteen feet tall. Where the trunk forks, a redcurrant bush has started to grow into the bark. A pair of wood pigeons sit in the tree a lot and they cheekily eat the redcurrants from the big bush further down. The seedling growing out of the elder tree was probably delivered as a seed via the pigeons.

May has its own unique vitality and energy. I always make sure I take time off work. The first full moon in May is very special to the Buddhists. It's when the Buddha was born, died and achieved enlightenment.

Wheels?

Wheels meaning that which gets you from A to B. One's motor. One's vehicle. One's mode of transport. The right vehicle is important up here. It has to negotiate the steep track and be able to carry loads of big heavy stuff. Our vehicles are a bit like our dogs – a reflection of our life-styles. (It's a red one).

When I came back from training school for the third year of my apprenticeship the firm had moved five miles further from home. I had to learn to drive and get a car. Getting the bus would have been just about possible, but it would have been pretty onerous.

Driving was different for teenagers when I started. It was affordable. Now insurance is prohibitively and obscenely expensive. When I took my driving test I didn't have a lot of confidence. On the way to the test centre, my instructor was covering his face, murmuring in a muffled scream, 'Watch that car!' I didn't hold out much hope.

At the end, I had to answer some Highway Code questions then suddenly out of the blue, the chap testing me said, 'I'm pleased to tell you that you've passed.' I couldn't believe my ears. It was my first attempt. I was only seventeen. I was on cloud nine for a month. It was a great confidence-booster. I probably looked about twelve when I passed my test. Understandably I was frequently stopped by the police. They always seemed to be rude and bullying. Maybe I was cheeky?

I have a childhood memory of lying in bed at night, imagining that I was flying a plane. I'd arranged my pillows around my head to create the cockpit. I've always had a certain *Boy's Own* love of classic well-built machinery – simple and functional – possible to repair without any fancy computerised gadgetry. Like a lot of lads, I was always building *Airfix* kits and oh how I adored the *Spitfire* and its incredible history[†]. I don't like the expanses of plastic in modern cars. I'm a fan of the elegance of 50s and 60s design. That type of styling in automotive engineering could never be replicated today, mainly due to safety restrictions.

My first car was a *Hillman Imp*. I saw it advertised in the local paper. I didn't have a clue what I should be looking for. I was ripped off. It was a pile of scrap. When my dad found out, he went into his smouldering rage mode, slipped his priest[*] into his pocket and came back with my money an hour later.

[†] I eventually wrote a song about the Spitfire called *Wake up Merlin* (as in Merlin engine).

[*] A priest is a small cosh that fishermen use for killing fish.

My dad kind of broke the mould. Hartleys before him were little and round. He was a six-foot-tall bruiser. He had his own gang as a boy and did stints as a boxer and a bouncer when he was in the air force. He joined when he was twenty-one and with the benefit of his engineering training, he worked in a squadron repairing and maintaining planes. He was sent off to college one day a week and got a Higher National Certificate (HNC) in engineering. He had a great time. He went back to being a toolmaker when he came out. In those days, an HNC was also a teaching qualification. He started teaching handicrafts at night school and ended up working at Pleckgate School in Blackburn. When Michael and I were little, he studied for a degree in history and economics at night through London University.

He eventually became head of handicrafts and economics. He was a great storyteller and could talk authoritatively about lots of subjects, especially history. He wasn't averse to a bit of bullshit and embellishment and loved embarrassing us in public by making loud pompous improbable statements. His greatest tales were from his own youth. In his late teens and before he joined the Air Force, he and his mates were off to the Yorkshire Dales caving and walking every weekend.

In one of his stories, he was challenged to a bare-knuckle fight by *The Champion of all Ireland and The North of England*. It took place under Ribblehead viaduct. They had a pint after every round until they were both absolutely plastered.

I remember one instance from our childhood when we were at our auntie's. A rather strait-laced couple were talking at length about the time and money they had spent on decorating. My dad suddenly announced, 'Anyone who wastes their time decorating is a complete and utter fool.' Many years later, I asked him about it. He remembered it well. He'd done it because the couple had insulted my mum which I hadn't picked up on at the time. He used to haggle with cashiers at supermarket tills. I truly believed that he was mentally retarded. I wonder where that authority-challenging bolshy streak of mine came from?

My kids never got into trouble but once when they were about ten or eleven, Elias and Sam were brought home by the police. Along with some of their errant mates, they'd been caught firing a BB gun* at passers-by. Later, we were visiting my dad's and I started telling him the tale. Their faces went pale with dread. My dad just said, 'So what, that's what they're for isn't it.' They broke into sweet little smiles and everyone laughed. We've all got a naughty streak.

---

* A BB gun is a low-powered air pistol that fires little yellow plastic pellets.

After the Imp debacle, my dad helped me look for a car. As it happens, a workmate of his had one for sale. It was a *Vauxhall Victor* – metallic gold and very 70s American. It was hard to work on. It had tiny little inaccessible spark plugs but it was pretty neat. The bonnet nearly flew off once when we were going to see *The Stray Cats* at Norbreck Castle in Blackpool. Learning to drive opened up my life. Now I could drive to gigs and go camping.

One day after work, my car wouldn't start. I went back into the tool room and found Grahame. 'Er, my car won't start.' He gave me the usual deadpan mock incredulity look and said, 'Well f'ing fix it then.' He then showed me how to jump-start it and he towed me round the yard – the battery was flat. Over the course of my apprenticeship, bit by bit they taught me how to fix cars. From then on I had a succession of old bangers and I kept them all going myself. Fixing old vehicles in the cold and wet became an affliction that I still haven't managed to cure.

My second-classiest car was a Triumph Herald. It was ace – a great design. I think the same chassis was used on some of their sports cars. It was nippy, economical and easy to work on. It had the tightest turning circle of any car of the time. My classiest car by far though was a Ford Consul Capri. It was tatty but magnificent and wonderful to drive. It was modelled off some of the big American coupés. Ford over-engineered it and lost money on it. I bought if off

Khany's mate Ken. Now Khany has a lovely metallic green one in America that he rebuilt himself. I had a go in it when me and the lads went to visit him. Mine broke down and it was in my dad's garage for ages until he forced me to sell it. The registration was 6BBU.

Notsensibles were mobile – four out of the five of us had cars. It was the norm for young working lads and lasses to save up and buy their own cars and drive. That was long before the criminal thieving insurance industry and its associated scams fucked it for ordinary young people. We all used to race home from rehearsals at Gary's. Rog had a Mini. Haggis had a brown Austin Allegro that I christened *The Turd on Wheels*, Kev had a Jag and I had my Capri. Khany has a beautiful faded photo of us all lined up in our cars outside Gary's. One of my great memories is of burning off Kev at the traffic lights at Casterton Avenue. I left him standing.

After my first few cars, I discovered the supreme folly of Morris Minors. I ran a succession of vans and Travellers right up until we moved up to Scotland when I went back to school. 1940s technology under a 1950s body. Why run something practical and comfortable when you can own an ancient unreliable dangerous expensive-to-run jalopy? That's me all over – at least 15 years behind. Perhaps the biggest Morris Minor van adventure was going to the last Stonehenge festival. Tom and I took turns at driving. I'd originally no intention of going, because the engine was knackered. I happened to have a spare one in my back yard. Our persuasive friend Martin Emmott said, 'Why don't we just change the engine?' This was the night before the solstice.

'You can't just swap an engine like that.'
'Why not?'
'It will take far too long.'
'No it won't.'

We had the engine in by dark and tuned it the next morning. Half a dozen of us set off in the afternoon and drove through the night. We arrived at dawn. Hawkind were playing and they were taking the piss out of *Coronation Street* actor William Roach – a druid. They were chanting, 'The great god Ken Barlow', with loads of repeating echo. It was very surreal. There were Quakers selling scrumpy. It was probably the last of the free festivals.

When the time came to move to Scotland it became apparent that enough was enough. After the first couple of times of rattling up and down the motorway in the old bone-shaker, I bought a very sensible and boring Ford Escort estate which I kept running for several years throughout medical school time. For once my years of messing about with cars paid off and I was able to maintain it cheaply.

I've always had estate cars or vans. It's part of the lifestyle. When the time came that I had enough money to buy an all round multi-purpose vehicle to suit my lifestyle, I finally chose something modern, comfortable and reliable. Right? Let's have a look at what's needed:

1. Enough ground clearance and low-end torque to get up the steep rough track to the ranch. Maybe a four-wheel drive?

2. Fits into a normal parking space and gets under car park height barriers.

3. Can fit a sheet of 8x4 ply in the back and 3.6 metre lengths of timber.

4. Can carry a band and all their gear to gigs.

5. Straightforward to self-maintain and all parts widely available.

6. Oh and you can live in it too.

7. Impeccable balance of iconic design and function. (How about a dinky pair of side patio-like doors that you can throw open with joyous abandon on arrival at a sunny campsite?)

Maybe you could call it a combination vehicle or even *Kombination* vehicle to make it sound trendy. Such a Tardis-like thing sounds impossible, but guess what, someone designed one in the 1950s and carried on making it until 1967. Amazingly, no-one else has had the sense to build a modern equivalent.

I have a thing about four-wheel drives and I have a special vernacular term for some of the high-end gas-guzzling giant ones. What's happened? Four-wheel drives used to be green and square and were used for carrying bales of straw.

As kids we used to play a game on motorway journeys making up words out of car number plates. Now the game is easily adaptable for modern times by making up more appropriate expletive titles from the letters of personalised number plates, signifying the gargantuan arrogance of the owner (inevitably driving a giant four-wheel drive). Anything with a 'C' in it is a gift.

Anyway, there I was looking round – studying the form – searching and researching. Eventually, typically for me, I bought a vehicle designed in the 1950s. I suppose it was a ten-year advance on Morris Minors – a step in the right direction. After a bit of rooting around on the internet, I got in touch with a chap in Cheshire who was importing these vehicles from South Africa. We went and had a look.

The one that he currently had up for sale was a bit scruffy-looking and over-priced but there was another one in the corner that had a certain charm about it. It had two inward-facing bench seats in the back which were both hinged and opened out into a bed. It had no MOT and needed a lot of work doing to get in on the road. 1965. German-built & assembled in South Africa. Right-hand drive. As ever, I was caught up in one of my unstoppable flights of folly and soon I'd negotiated a price if he would get it MOT'd and on the road.

Six weeks later and it was ready. I let the lads have a day off school and we set off on the train to pick it up. The alarm bells should have started ringing straight away when I noticed that they had removed a rather sweet little non-original temperature gauge from the dashboard. When I asked about it, they assured me that I was mistaken. I pulled out the photographs that I'd taken on the day that we bought it and showed them the one of the dash clearly showing the gauge in position. They laughed and squirmed then made up some bullshit excuse that they had got mixed up with another one that they'd just sold. I also noticed that the MOT was from a garage several miles away.

We set off in it, and it was utterly terrifying to drive. The steering was incredibly sloppy and the engine was coughing and spluttering. Fortunately, it broke down a mile down the road. I didn't fancy driving any further with my kids in it. I phoned up the vendors and they came and picked us up and promised to sort it and deliver it to my house. They dropped us off at the train station.

Weeks later, they delivered it. I started going through the mechanics and it became immediately apparent that no way on earth should it have got through an MOT. They were crooks and I could have got my money back. Despite all this though, it was a reasonably straight right-hand drive example which are increasingly rare and expensive.

I'd always had a soft spot for VW split-screens. We were once at the Tate gallery in London. I walked round a corner and there was a real-life full size one pulling a load of sledges. It looked so beautiful and well-designed. Not too big. Not too small – a perfection of poise and elegance. It was an exhibit by *Joseph Beouys*. He'd driven it for years then turned it into a piece of art. I wasn't interested in the sledges. I spent ages studying the impeccable details of the van.

Years before that, there was a second-hand shop in Tod called *Jack Pepper's*. We once bought a big mirror there to go over the fireplace at the old house. There was always a tatty split-screen parked outside and it just looked so neat. I have a thing about bench seats and split-screens have them – three people can sit in the front. Maybe there's something about the stark functionality of the driving compartment that makes me think I'm flying a World War two aeroplane – the dinky little row of three square side windows is certainly reminiscent of a plane.

So began a long saga that warrants a book in itself:

Owning a VW split-screen in the 21st century – the truth, the whole truth and nothing but the truth.

Having a vehicle that is infinitely repairable does have appeal. We're conditioned to get another car every few years. Long-term repair and maintenance doesn't fit into today's consumerist society – so much so in fact, that it's impossible to repair modern cars yourself – you have to plug them into a computer in order to be told that some complicated electronic device has expired and must be replaced at astonishing expense. Split-screens are so popular that you can get any part for them and most towns have someone who specialises in them. Having said that, my enthusiasm for lying underneath mine in the cold and wet is all but exhausted.

I've lost count of the number of times that it's broken down. A large number of these breakdowns were during my kids' most sensitive years and the humiliation of them having to push it for long distances in public was at times particularly acute.

Despite all this, so far it has fulfilled its purpose. My aim was always to use it as an all-round workhorse vehicle whilst slowly restoring it and I've managed to achieve this at least in part. I've replaced all the running gear. It has a new bog-standard 1600 engine and a taller gear box so it will cruise comfortably on the motorway. A stainless exhaust and twin carbs give it a bit of extra oomph.

The inward-facing bench seats makes for the most sociable possible set-ups in a split. A few years ago six of us drove all the way to Southern Ireland in it for my friend Dewy's stag do. Miraculously, it never broke down. The night before getting the ferry from Holyhead, we met up with another bunch of friends on their way to the do and ten of us had a party in the van (including musical instruments). It has carried vast quantities of sand, cement, timber and myriad gardening sundries to the ranch up a track where only Land Rovers dare.

We've been on numerous holidays and camping trips in it and to lots of festivals. When it comes to camping, rain or shine, there is simply no finer vehicle on earth. Nothing can beat the way those little side doors open out. I never use an awning – that would defeat the object. We take a separate little tent instead. If it's raining, we have a camouflage tarpaulin that we rig up as a little porch using two tent poles. It stops water dripping in.

When camping, I sleep diagonally on the rearward facing seat in the back which has a z-hinge, and opens out flat. I take three pillows and two sheepskins to go under my luxury double sleeping bag. During the day, the bed transforms into a very comfortable lounging area. The rear bench seat makes a nice settee and the space in the back makes a perfect little kitchen. I've made a small table that sits snugly against the side. I have an original sixties Blaupunkt radio in the front and I've adapted the auxiliary socket to take an iPod. All in all it's a rather civilised affair. When not in use, the camping gear is stored in the cellar and the attic and is fairly easy to load for a trip. A camping conversion means permanently carrying a lot of extra weight. I prefer to maximise the versatility.

I camp in the van at the most ten days a year. Each camping trip is a little holiday and before we set off, we stock up on the most luxurious of food items and the finest ales and wines. Standard items include fresh ground coffee in the mornings and the ability to cook pizza (a combination of a hotplate over one of the gas rings and the grill).

At festivals, I camp as far away as possible from the din. The lads (and their three or four mates who always came with us) used to take their tents and camp in the Babylonian hub. Latterly, they've realised that being in the proximity of the abject luxury that the van affords is more advantageous and relaxing. I used to frequently return from a walkabout to find several of them partying or sleeping (depending on the time of the day). Typically, they would come back to the van every few hours and eat gargantuan amounts of food. Partying in the van is often more fun than the festival itself.

One year, we went to the *Kendal Calling* music festival. My two lads Sam and Elias and their friend Matt and I set off the night before. We camped on a beautiful little site by a pub at the top of Thirlmere, a few miles away from the festival. I left the lads to pitch their tent as I went on a reconnaissance mission to investigate the hostelry. Later we had a lovely meal outside the pub in the evening sun.

The next morning, we departed at 8.00 am in plenty of time to get into the festival early doors. About a mile down the road, the van spluttered to a halt. I opened the engine lid at the back and there were black flakes of something in the petrol filter.

The night before, we'd had an altercation with an ape-like couple who had asked us to turn our night heater off because the fumes were going into their tent. I'd explained that it wasn't a night heater (it's an *Eberspacher*, piped into the petrol tank) and that I'd switch it off. I also told them that it took about five minutes to burn the residual fuel in the system before the heater switched itself off. They came back two minutes later and were quite rude, so I gave them both barrels of my rapier wit. I was showing off a bit to the lads. Black flakes in the fuel filter? I was suspecting that when we repaired to the hostelry for a bite to eat, they'd put something in the petrol tank. The plugs were covered in soot. I cleaned them and replaced the in-line filter before we managed to limp another few yards then the same thing happened. Over the next couple of hours, we stumbled along a few yards at a time and managed to get into Threlkeld. I had a hunch that it was probably something simple, but I just couldn't work it out.

Another hour went by and the lads got fed up. They got their camping equipment and got the bus to Penrith, then hitch-hiked to the festival. They could only carry their tents and sleeping bags and left their beer behind. Taking some food didn't even cross their minds.

I found a garage up the road and they were very helpful, but still I couldn't fix the problem. I knew it wasn't the air filters because I'd only cleaned them the week before. The chap at the garage very kindly said that I could park there overnight – he used to know my friend Chris from Keswick. Small world. It started getting late, and there was a campsite across the road so I headed for that. After an hour or so of sputtering to a halt every few yards and cleaning the plugs three times, I finally made it. I set up camp for the night. As it started going dark, the fine weather gave way to a persistent heavy drizzle (PHD). Sam had left his iPod in the van. I had a large array of luxury food items and top quality French wine to hand. I was stranded but stranded in style.

It would have been dead easy to call the breakdown company but I was still hoping to make it to the festival. The next morning I rigged up the tarpaulin over the back (it was still PHDing non-stop) and I stripped down the carbs and replaced all the fuel lines (I speculated that the black flakes in the petrol filter could have come from a disintegrating fuel pipe). I started the engine again – no change. It spluttered to a halt after a couple of minutes. I gave up for the day and went for a long walk in the grey drizzle along deserted winding roads. I watched a red deer grazing towards me along the edge of a forest, oblivious of my presence. I'd phoned the lads the night before and they'd arrived safely.

It was a kind of a contemplative experience. It almost reminded me of the *Family Guy* episode when Brian and Stewy got locked in a bank vault overnight. I kept going over and over in my head what the problem with the van might be:

Petrol tank (fuel pipes replaced); carbs (stripped, cleaned and replaced); engine (running fine). It had to be the petrol. I decided that I would walk into Keswick the next day and try and get some. In the meantime, I cooked a leisurely evening meal. The next morning, bolstered by a fine breakfast of bacon, sausage, tomatoes, egg, mushrooms and beans, book-ended by two cups of the finest milky coffee, I set off for Keswick. There was a sun-filled break in the rain and I followed the stunning path which follows the river Greta – a magnificent walk. I had a leisurely look round Keswick then I bought a petrol can at the ironmonger's and a gallon of petrol at the garage.

Chris had left his farmhouse in Keswick many years ago and had moved to live with his mum and sister in Spain. Sadly he died when he was out there. I had been to Keswick a few times since to visit his son but it wasn't the same. It's not the little Lakeland market town that it used to be. It's crammed with outdoor shops, its charm squashed by uber-tourism. It was too late to start working on the van by the time I got back. The day had enjoyed a brief warm sunny reprise but the PHD had now settled in for the night. Besides, I had a meal to cook and a cheeky *Chateauneuf du Pape* to investigate. Phone signals were poor but I managed to get through to Sam briefly. Things didn't sound too rosy. They had run out of money and they were cold, wet and hungry. I could sense a *Lord of the Flies* desperation.

I was camped in a small field at the far end of the site enjoying the exquisite solitude. As dusk drew in, I watched a family arrive in a silver Land Rover – they drove around and around the field a few times, then came and parked right next to me and started pitching their tent. It's incredible how some people have no sense of personal space. They were loud Geordies. They clearly weren't experienced campers. It was pissing with rain and their tent was blowing all over the place – they didn't have a clue.

After fifteen minutes of being a grumpy twat, I pulled myself together and went and helped them. I realised that my arrogant interpretation of 'personal space' was wrong. They were clearly a bit nervous about camping for the first time (in the rain) and felt safer being close to another camper.

Once their tent was up, I invited them into the van and gave the bloke an ale and his wife some vino. I made hot chocolate for the two kids – a boy and a girl aged about nine and ten.

The next morning, their cooker wasn't working. I boiled a kettle for them and suggested that they drive into Keswick and I'd watch the kids. I made them some breakfast and we played catches in the rain. When the couple got back, the bloke kindly offered to drive me to a town if I needed any parts. It was Sunday morning and the rolling grey threatening clouds suddenly gave way to a sunny sky and a warm breeze.

Using a funnel and a length of fuel pipe I bypassed the petrol tank and poured in some of the new petrol. I turned the key and the engine started and ran sweetly until the fuel in the funnel ran out. Hallelujah! Sorted. All I needed to do now was drain the petrol tank, put in the new petrol and hey presto I would be back on the road. So I was right, the fuel was contaminated. What with though? Had they put sugar in the tank? I was hoping that the engine wasn't ruined.

I reconnected the fuel supply to the petrol tank and just before draining it, I thought I'd see if it would start. It did. I waited for it to splutter to a halt after a few minutes but it didn't. Now I was puzzled. It seemed that the petrol tank wasn't contaminated after all. I thought I'd give it a run and see what happened so I put the air filters back on and drove round the campsite – once again it spluttered to a halt and in an instant I knew what the problem was. After all that it was the air filters. I cleaned them in petrol and everything was fine.

I vaguely recall reading *Zen in The Art of Motorcycle Maintenance*. It was a long time ago and I can't remember much about it but the gist was that there's a strong relationship between maintaining a vehicle and getting your head together. There's something inexplicably rewarding about laying out your tools and planning a job on your vehicle then carrying it out successfully. When there's a problem, there's a certain type of mental investigation required which is quite stimulating. In this case, the lesson was that if you do something incredibly fucking stupid for long enough, life will eventually and unavoidably, give you the lessons that you need. My *Zen in the art* inevitably involves a certain amount of *Don Quixote-Rocinante* delusion. Here was some salutary learning. It was nothing to do with the apes. My bombastic presumption had blinded me to a very simple and obvious problem. But where had the black flakes in the fuel filter come from? How come the air filters had clogged up so soon after I'd cleaned them?

I later found out that VW air-cooled engines can create a lot of oily mist in the engine compartment. You can solve the problem by relieving the pressure in the rocker box covers with a pipe to a filter. I replaced the small mesh air filters with two huge K&N race filters at the earliest opportunity.

By now, I'd had enough. I just wanted to go home. I packed up and said goodbye to the Geordie family. I gingerly headed south and was soon on the A66. I stopped once to tweak the carbs and hey presto, the van was running better than ever. It was around lunchtime. I could be on the ranch by mid-afternoon. I didn't have much sympathy for the lads. They were the ones who buggered off and left me. It would do them good to find their own way home.

I don't know what made me change my mind, but I did. I turned round and headed north again. Just before Keswick there's a long steep rise in the road. As I began to climb it, I could see a bay* in the distance. I slowly caught up with it, sat behind it for a couple of minutes, then slid past up the hill and left it standing. Standard VW split screens are pretty slow but with my modest modifications, mine is faster than most splits and bays.

I stopped off at Booth's in Keswick and stocked up on a large array of indulgence food. Pop, crisps, cheeses, nice bread, cakes. A quick blast up to Penrith and down a couple of B roads and I was there. What a lovely place.

The festival takes place in Lowther Deer Park. It was now hot and sunny. There was lots of room in the camper-van field. I set up the little folding table and chairs and tried ringing Sam but his phone was dead. (I've fitted a cigarette lighter in the van and I carry a 12-volt phone charger). I tried a few other numbers and finally got through to Tyler.

'I'm here. I'm in the camper van field.'
'Oh – right, we'll come round.'

---

* 'Bay' refers to the 'bay window' VW transporter which superseded the split screen in 1968. Although bays are iconic vehicles in their own right, they come nowhere near the split-screen in terms of superlative design and desirability.

Tyler is a brilliant drummer and plays in a band with Elias, Sam and Matt. He'd made his own way to the festival. Normally at festivals, they saunter up to the van at the most casual of paces. Today though, they were sprinting so fast that they ran right past before they saw it.

We had an extended feast and exchanged tales of the last two days then went and caught the last of the music. I saw one of the best drummers I'd ever seen, playing with a funky-sounding jazz band. The next day, we had a leisurely uneventful journey home. There was plenty of ripe fruit to pick on the ranch. There are numerous good reasons why the VW Kombi is one of the most iconic vehicles ever made. It has a certain perfection of form and function that is difficult to fully describe. I'm at a crossroads at the moment. Shall I bite the bullet and do the front-end rebuild needed for the next MOT or shall I sell it and get something modern & sensible? We'll see.

9. Dog

Table, top of ranch. Friday 15th May.

A squashed-faced, baldy, bow-legged cunt comes waddling around the corner and sure enough, the owner, following close behind has similar characteristics.

What is it with the English and their dogs? The beasts are somehow extensions of what we imagine ourselves to be. Young lads with vicious fighting dogs. Petite women with cuddly little yapping lap dogs. Improbable breeds with improbable names; what's going on?

We never had a dog when we were kids because my mum didn't like them but our childhood was filled with colourful memories of my dad's accounts of his lurcher Gerry. When he was about ten years old, he and his friend Jimmy Waddington found a litter of pups under a hen hut. They were all dead except for two. They took one each. My dad's mum would never have allowed him to have a dog. She was a weaver and my grandad was a driver. Times then were hard and it was unthinkable for ordinary working class people to have any spare cash to feed a pet.

Lurchers were bred originally for hunting small game at a time when hunting was strictly illegal for all but the gentry. Typically a lurcher is a cross between a sight hound (usually a greyhound) and another working dog – often a terrier or sheepdog or strains of both.

My dad hid the dog in the air raid shelter and fed him milk from a bottle. Of course he was soon caught. The dog was slowly and reluctantly accepted by his mum and dad but not by his grandma. Gerry telepathically knew when the fierce merciless woman was about to arrive and would scuttle out of the back door sharpish. A dog in a house? Unthinkable for a farming woman.

My dad also kept ferrets and bred mice. How lovely – they could all play together. Actually not. A dog had to earn its keep. The mice fed the ferrets and the ferrets went down the rabbit holes and the dog picked up any rabbits that escaped the nets. Butchers paid good money for rabbits and they made an excellent family meal at a time when people were genuinely poor and sometimes went hungry.

My dad had loads of anecdotes about Gerry: Returning with a pie in his mouth (people used to put pies on window sills to cool); ripping up his posh friend Raymond's gloves; coming home with a corset in his mouth and keeping it in his basket for ever thereafter; religiously coming upstairs and nuzzling him awake early every Saturday morning to go rabbiting along the railway; jumping over the same bridge that he's jumped over hundreds of times only to discover that the river had dried up during the hot dry summer (he was uninjured); running to greet my dad many years later when he returned from the air force on leave (Gerry lived to be 19).

My dad's storytelling came into its own and these tales struck a chord with my own kids. One day when Louise read out an advert in the local paper: *Lurcher pups for sale.* Their imagination was captured and they went a bit crazy – 'We'll look after him, we'll pay for him.' (but you don't have any money). They were about 6, 8 and 13 at the time. They phoned my dad and they scrabbled down the back of the settee and in their bedrooms looking for money. Unfortunately, having a dog wasn't an option at the time. I was doing lots of nights and lots of commuting and it would fall to Louise to feed and take it out. The answer was a definite no. They even rang me up at work: 'Can we just go and have a look?'

The dog came from an allotment over the other side of the hill from mine. He was from a long line of rabbiters. He was riddled with fleas – a tiny black bundle with a white chest – we called him Jet. He could just about walk, but he kept falling over and I wondered if the fleas had made him anaemic. We put him in the kitchen and when we came down in the morning, he'd disappeared. We found him cowering inside the legs of the drop-leaf table. For the next few nights, the lads insisted on sleeping in the kitchen with him to keep him company. We had to wait for his injections to take effect before we took him out for the first time. When we did, he was terrified, nuzzling against my legs and whimpering to be picked up. He soon got used to it.

He grew into the sleekest fastest lurcher that I've ever seen. We're fortunate to live on the edge of a park with lots of flat open spaces where he could sprint freely. People would often stop and enquire 'Does he do owt?' (meaning does he catch rabbits). The best compliment he ever got though was from a lurcher breeder: 'That cunt's well muscled up.' I used to play chases with him on the golf course early in the morning and late in the evening when there were no golfers about. I would chase him and he would chase me – of course he could run three times faster. There are lots of drainage channels that we would both jump over. I trained him to heel by walking with him on the lead. Every time he tried to pull, I swung a carrier bag in front of his nose and stopped. He quickly got the hang of it. I also trained him to not go near sheep using a long lead. As he first darted to chase them, I would quickly pull him back and say, 'no' very firmly. He was a quick learner. The kids used to have one of those giant skate boards and he would pull them along on it.

We were once on holiday camping at Kirkby Lonsdale. We were walking through a sloping field with the dog and there was a herd of cows at the top quite a distance away. They suddenly charged at us. They thundered down the hill and they were gaining on us quickly as we tried to make the stile in the bottom corner of the field. I thought we were all going to be crushed in the stampede. Jet broke away and ran towards them with his nose to the ground. He then just lay down facing them and miraculously they stopped and we escaped. Clearly he has some sheepdog in him.

One of the greatest achievements of my medical career happened when Jet got a nasty cut on his paw from a piece of glass – it was about two inches long. The kids and their mates held him down and I sutured it, using local anaesthetic and stitches from the first aid kit that I used to carry, thus avoiding a hefty vet's bill.

He's getting on a bit now. He's the most gentle and humble of dogs. Can dogs be polite? Ours is. He hardly ever barks and if he wants to come into a room he quietly taps on the door. How come so many humans have pet dogs? Love and companionship perhaps? It's good to teach children to respect animals. Human beings can be broadly divided into those who are cruel to animals and those who aren't.

Jet is very wary around other male dogs. When he was not much more than a puppy he was attacked by another lurcher called Sandy. Sandy didn't just attack him once – he attacked him several times. His irresponsible owner had him off the lead and couldn't control him. Sam was probably about eleven when he was out one day with his friend Jack. He had Jet on the lead. Suddenly Sandy attacked. It was the last time. Sam couldn't keep hold of Jet and a vicious fight ensued – apart from a scratch, Jet was uninjured. We never saw Sandy again.

I was up at five this morning. I've been out 'rabbiting' in the park with Jet. It's now 9.30 and I'm on the ranch. The weather is beautiful – cloudy and breezy with patches of sun. The trees are mostly in leaf and the tall Valerian at the bottom is on the verge of releasing its heady scent. I've loads of plants in propagators – courgettes, beans, onions, peas, beetroot and loads more on the concrete at the top hardening off.

Jet doesn't like it up here. Every time I move, he jumps up and sidles towards the door. He's giving me that mournful 'Take me home fucker' look. He's adopted a pose of abject misery – slightly cowed with his tail between his legs.

'Can't you see how miserable I am? Take me home you twat.'

There's a saying that lurchers can stand any amount of luxury and it's true. For his first few years, he wasn't allowed on the furniture but that sort of went by the wayside. He can happily occupy a full two-seater settee. His full relaxation pose is lying on his back, legs in air, and balls on show.

One cold winter day, I'd just come in and I went upstairs to lie down. I noticed that my side of the bed was warm and I presumed that Louise had left the electric blanket on. She hadn't. On close inspection, there was a bit of an indentation and some dog hair. He must have shot downstairs sharpish when he heard me coming in. What a cheek. He'd never been allowed upstairs.

When I say 'rabbiting' he doesn't actually catch any. This morning we crept onto the edge of the pitch-and-putt course which was swarming with rabbits. I pointed his head in the direction of one just ten yards away and gently nudged him. Off he went. He swiftly caught up with it but then shame of shame, he ran a circle around it and barked. He was once hit by a motorbike that some kids were riding in the park. I reckon it gave him brain damage. Apparently a hunting lurcher has to be 'bloodied' as part of its training – local rabbiters usually get the dog to kill a pet rat to get the taste for blood. Jet was a pet so we never did that – he did once find a rat under a sheet of plastic down at the bottom of the ranch, but he didn't have the instinct to harm it.

Once when he was out with Rachel and Louise, he came out of the bushes with what looked like a dead rabbit in his mouth. They screamed at him to put it down and it ran off unharmed.

There are a pair of crows that come with us on the dog walk. We give them crushed dog biscuits. I don't know how it started. They're very clever. They recognise me even when I don't have the dog. Life is like the dog walk sometimes. All you need are shite bags, biscuits and a lead.

What kind of dog am I?

I'm a lurcher of course. There's definitely some sheepdog in there. I'm probably a whippet cross. Then there's that streak of pig-headed tenacity that just never gives up – not sure where that comes from.

10. Rock & Roll 2
...including the joy of the 7" single.

Friday 29th May. Table, top of ranch.

I'm up on this hill again, farther and farther from the madding crowd. I'm proud of my minority-of-one credentials. I'm too fussy and uncompromising. I'd rather be up here in solitude than be pimping myself to buffoons. I'm losing all desire for peopled places. The fleeting presence of the blackbirds and sparrows is preferable to enduring the uncomfortable company of narrow-minded dicks, fucktards and rude cunts. Is there such a thing as intellectual loneliness? In the eyes of those around me, having an allotment is at best a bit of a hippy-dippy hobby whereas to me it's the fundamental foundation of a way of life that stands aside from the insanity of our current society. Growing clean food is the first building block.

'Ooh that's a nice hobby – so long as you have a proper job as well.' They can all fuck off even though they're probably right.

Sometimes I'm like the spoilt child running away from home with my handkerchief tied into a bundle. I like to fantasise that I have everything I need up here. I can camp in the van if I want to.

The sweet air of late May fills my lungs and the rampant vibrant growth all around exudes an invisible joy and energy. My grumpiness dissolves and my twat tantrum runs its course. I don't need a medical research project to tell me that this kind of environment is good for my health.

It's raining a soft fine penetrating drizzle (FPD) but it really doesn't matter. I don't pay much attention to weather forecasts. I can feel a warm radiant glow beyond the grey canopy and I just know that it's going to fine up later.

I do my exercises. I have a daily routine which I've done for years ever since I slipped a disc. It borrows from the warm up that we used to do at kung fu and involves stretching every joint through its full range of movement. I'm sure that exercising to the maximum of your ability is good for your health – particularly if it's outdoors. Going to the gym would be a punishment for me; breathing in a mist of sweat, skin flakes and toxic aluminium compounds in the company of flabby narcissists. Horses for courses.

I always carry a bag when I come up here. I bring empty bottles, bricks, screws, nails, packed lunches and I take back fruit and veg and firewood.

The neurotic male blackbird gives his usual chattering display every time I walk anywhere near his wife on her nest and the robin darts about as usual eyeing me suspiciously and it's all OK. The tufty pale pink valerian flowers are now open, giving off their exquisite musky perfume. The plant goes from strength to strength – it's nearly seven feet tall.

As soon as I take something out of a propagator, I try and fill the space immediately with more seeds in trays. Planting small amounts regularly seems to work well. Today I'm planting coriander, dill, parsley and beetroot. Beetroot grows virtually all year round so I always have a few seedlings on the go to fill the gaps when other stuff comes out. This year I've tried marjoram, marsh mallow and *Artemisia annua,* all of which are coming on nicely. For years, I've been building up a repertoire of plants that I can collect seed from and grow in decent quantities, in anticipation of doing plant sales.

It's daft that I still don't have a greenhouse after all this time. I'm relying on four propagators made from slate baton and clear polycarbonate sheeting. Like so many other jobs and projects, it's on the list. Like life in general, when there's more work to be done than you can possibly have time for, you have to prioritise. At this time of year planting and gardening take priority although I'm still doing a bit of concreting and building as well.

I'm thinking about music again. Snobs like me slag off the majority of commercial music. Music is music though and if it brings some joy to the performer or listener then fine. Personally I believe in Rock & Roll pure, passionate and visceral like it was when it first emerged from black America all those years ago. Not for me the bland banal over-worked middle-of-the-road insipid bilge that haunts our airwaves these days.

'When the fish scent fills the air, there'll be snuff juice everywhere.'
'... like a one-eyed jack, peeping in the sea-food store.' *

What's all that about? Angry, irreverent, smoulderingly sexual, outrageous but spare me mediocrity – I can cope

---

* *Wang Dang Doodle* written by Willie Dixon for Howling Wolf and recorded on Chess in 1960 – recorded by Koko Taylor in 1964. *Shake, Rattle and Roll* written in 1954 by Jesse Stone and originally recorded by Big Joe Turner and most successfully by Bill Haley and his Comets. Elvis did a great version.

with anything except mediocrity. Give me the Northern post-punk songwriting ethic anytime. Cryptic auto-biography and so on. I like cryptic. A lot of art, music and romance relies on cryptic, not to mention spiritual teaching. Hint and innuendo and a sly smile here and there – what's wrong with that? We don't always have to spell everything out.

I'm not mega keen on saxophones and mouth organs. The strumming singer-songwriter is not my cup of tea. When it comes to guitar sound, I'm an uber-purist. Only valve amps will do. I ended up building my own.

I saw the first line-up of The Fall. I saw The Stray Cats at Norbreck Castle. I saw The Birthday Party at The Hacienda – all good examples. So too are Hamburg Beatles, 50s Elvis, Mick Taylor period Stones. I like guitar music in a sparse and simple setting – Hendrix, Stray Cats, G-love and Special sauce and a lot of the genuine early rhythm and blues. Add a horn section, and that pretty much includes soul and funk too. I love the pure rockabilly stuff – Gene Vincent's first two albums with Cliff Gallup on guitar – early Elvis with Scotty Moore on guitar.

A mark of a great band is that they have a live recording somewhere that matches their studio output in quality. My 'gold standard' live performance is Hendrix playing *Voodoo Child* on the Lulu show. Another is Bowie's *Oh You Pretty*

Things on The Old Grey Whistle test. Bill Wither's laid back *Ain't no sunshine when she's gone* – also from The Whistle test. *Drink that Bottle Down* by The Stray Cats is brilliant and *The High Numbers* at The Railway is a corker. I adore The *Beatles Live at The Star Club Hamburg* and *The Million Dollar Quartet* recordings are pretty much my favourite ever. Carl Perkins' guitar sound is exquisite. Most of the early Rock & Roll and Rhythm & Blues was recorded live anyway.

A lot of guitarists are dicks. They have a compulsive urge to twat about then turn up as loudly as possible and completely drown out the rest of the band. No amount of reasoning will cure them of their malady. It's a deep-rooted mental condition and I confess that I've been guilty at times. Nowadays, if I see a band go on stage then start dicking about and twiddling before they play, they're off my list for good. The worst crime of all is playing along to the jukebox – instant dismissal. As for twiddling during a recording session – that's a complete non-starter. No surprise then that since Notsensibles, I've played almost exclusively in 3-piece bands – just one dick guitarist (me) and a bassist and a drummer.

The exception was the two-piece with Tom. At our pinnacle, we played at *The Everyman* theatre in Liverpool. We were supporting *Martin Demi-god's* band – I can't remember their name. After we played, I was approached by Bunnymen guitarist *Will Sergeant.* He wanted to buy my guitar. No chance – it was my wonderful sparkly-white *Eko* with four pickups and a row of white sliders. *Ticker le punk* loves it and has been trying to get it off me for years. At the same gig we were approached by a woman who wanted to manage us. She was blown away and reckoned we could be successful but obscurity beckoned and it never happened.

Ticker is a couple of years younger than me. He wears well co-ordinated outfits with a punk theme invariably topped with a hat. He talks in a low quiet fast voice and a lot of people can't tell a word that he's saying which can be very funny at times. He used to go to The Railway Workers and later The Carlton. For many years The Carlton was the music pub where all the punky types, bohos and misfits hung out. There were bands and DJs on every week. It's long-gone now. The smoking ban killed it. Ticker is a punk aficionado with encyclopaedic knowledge not only of punk but also most other music. In any conversation he will say, 'Have you heard of... by...' then reel off loads of obscure records by bands that hardly anyone has ever heard of. We're both big vinyl fans and we DJ together sometimes. We largely stick to 7" singles. One of our finest moments was un-witnessed. It was at *Beatherder* festival in the early hours of the morning after a heavy night. I was playing Notsensibles songs on my guitar and Ticker was rapping over the top in the most hilarious manner. Ticker is kind to animals and has a razor sharp wit. Elias and I bumped into him in The Bridge last week and he had us in stitches. He made a hilarious quip about the yuppies of Hebden Bridge paying a hundred quid a pop to get their cats' beards trimmed.

Up until relatively recently, every hit record without exception came out on 7" single. The seven-inch single was the currency of Rock & Roll, the currency of pop, the currency of punk and just about every other genre of music up until the early eighties. I suppose The Smiths were the last real singles band before digital got its hooks in. All true-blooded musos have record players. There's no exception to that rule. You sometimes come across people who claim to be DJs but then it turns out that they don't have a record player or any records (DJ stands for <u>disc</u> jockey, dick). A few months ago we went to *Band on The Wall* for Tricia's birthday. There was a well known 'DJ' on but he was just tapping a laptop and waving his arms in the air. It was shite. There's always some histrionic drama on our nights out where one of us has a drunken strop. This time it was a stupid argument about page 3 girls.

Collecting 7" singles is a bit like stamp collecting. There's a nerdy element to it. There's the back story – the history of the band – where the record was recorded etc. Then there's the record itself – the label, the sleeve and finally there's the music. Often you'll find a B-side that's better than the A-side – *I'm Leaving* (B-side of Boom Boom) by John Lee

Hooker for example. Ticker and I will sometimes buy a single just because the label looks interesting and we've never seen it before. We ran a monthly 7" singles club night for a while.

I have my singles organised in genres: soul; R&B & mod; funk and funky; jazz and cheerful and cheesy; 60s; 1974 onwards. There's no perfect filing system. Sometimes a single can belong to up to three genres, making things tricky. My A-list singles are in the old-fashioned square boxes. There are loads more on shelves. I've released four 7" singles so far on my little label. I came up with a sleeve design reminiscent of 60s *Brunswick* and *London*, then cut it into a woodblock. Every year at midnight at our New Year's Eve party, I play Jackie Wilson's (*Your Love Keeps Lifting me) Higher and Higher* then quickly flip it over and play *The Sweetest Feeling*. It's an example of what I call a PALG single – pure absolute liquid gold. Everything about it is perfect – the Brunswick company sleeve, the label, the recording, the songs. It was my friends Taff and Fran's going out record when they were teenagers.

It's only relatively recently that I've started getting into Northern Soul. That's a musical genre based entirely and exclusively on 7" singles. I already had quite a few Northern records that I didn't even know were Northern – it's all American R&B to me. I was DJing one night and someone asked me if I'd play some more Northern soul – I didn't realise that I'd been playing it in the first place. A typical example is Jimmy Robbin's *I Can't Please You* – to my ears, it's stomping R&B but apparently it's a big Northern track. I've analysed it and realised that the common theme is a characteristic *chugga chugga* rhythm often with a staccato *chic chic* in the background.

The guitarist in the covers band that Tom played in (Victor Drago) when I met him was Gary Lomax – a master of the surreal and unusual. I first saw them play at *The Rifle Volunteers* in Rossendale. Gary taught photography and produced great photo-montages long before the digital age. He once made a 12" single as *The Waterfoot Dandy*. At The Volunteers he was wearing eye liner and had one of his front teeth blacked out. He was playing the most beautiful guitar that I'd ever seen in my life – it was a red double-cutaway semi – wafer thin and a perfection of aesthetic poise and elegance – far more beautiful than the similar but uglier Gibson ES335. It was a *Hofner Verithin*. He was playing it through a 60s blonde *Fender Tremolux* and a crocodile skin *Selmer* cab. It looked and sounded awesome. 'One day,' I thought. 'One day'.

A few months later outside the same pub, a bunch of lads started on our friend Michael Spencer. His smouldering sultry good looks and brooding contemplation were often misinterpreted for aggression. I was just setting off in my car at the time to go home. In the excitement, I stalled and bumped into the wall. It was my beautiful blue *Triumph Herald*. I had some good adventures in that car. In a trice, *Alice Nutter* – then in her ultra-punky phase with spiky blonde hair and fishnet stockings, ran out of the pub, took off her studded belt and took on the lot of them – they were shit-scared and sloped off.

The two-piece was actually the leftovers from a much larger sprawling band called *Ow! My hairs on fire are you bothered?* – we only did a couple of gigs. There was me, Tom, Alice, Michael Spencer, Simon Kember and a few other floating members including Spider. Simon's mum and dad had a wonderful old farmhouse in Britannia. We used to rehearse in the barn and all camp there when they went on holiday. Good times. We didn't last long. Alice went off and joined Chumbawamba.

I mentioned that I met Fenny when I was busking outside M&S. I did a fanzine at the time that I printed in my kitchen. It was the days of *Letraset*, glue and photocopiers, long before the digital age. He started writing a column for it. Every time an issue came out, I used to go on the weekly indie show[*] at the local radio station and talk about it. Steve Barker ran the programme (and still does). As

---

[*] The show was originally called *RPM* and then *Spin-off* before morphing into *On The Wire*. It's the longest-running BBC radio of its kind, on the air for over 30 years.

ever, he was always very supportive. Fenny started doing a slot on the programme as a progression of his fanzine column and he's still doing it. He blames me for getting him on the radio. One day – long after the two-piece had split up and I was hankering for a band again, I phoned Fenny out of the blue. 'Me, thee and Tom', were my actual words. He was a bit taken aback because he didn't play an instrument. I think he was chuffed to play in his first band at the age of forty. He learned to play my old Stu Sutcliffe bass and we had a great couple of years. We did quite a few gigs and we recorded an album – in fact we recorded two versions. We were called *The Three Platitudes* – I thought it was a great name.

Tom worked at The *Abraham Moss Centre* in Manchester and he had use of the recording studio in the evenings whenever it was free. We recorded one album in the 8 track studio and the other in the 24 track studio. We even played at The Edinburgh festival in a small hut off the beaten track. The comedian *Rory Motion* was top of the bill. We never got round to releasing the album.

Tom later went on to record as *Mrs Cakehead*, with an electro-ragga style backing, and his hilarious lyrics over the top. He did a brilliant EP which was the first release on my record label. One of my favourite lyrics of all time from one of the songs on the EP is 'Foul denizens of Burnley.'

Not long after that, I started medical school and we had two young children. Looking back, I was a bit fucked and had turned into even more of a twat. When the time came to start my first job as a house officer I was shit scared. I retired from music and sold my beloved beige AC30 and the Stu Sutcliffe bass which I'd bought off one of *The Mirror Boys* in Leeds for fifty quid. I declined to take part in a Notsensibles reunion. I was too twitched about entering the rat race. I was also thinking that punk was a movement of youthful rebellion and reunions for forty-year-olds were purely cabaret.

I sold the bass to the music shop on the corner of our street for fifty quid. I immediately regretted it. I put the Vox AC30 in the local paper – they're one of the most iconic guitar amps ever made. They had a brief slump in popularity when transistor amps came in but had become iconic again when I had mine. Brian May used huge banks of them. Before that, lots of famous 60's bands had used them – The Beatles, The Stones. They were covered in black vinyl. Mine was beige so I presumed that it had been re-covered and was a bit of a duffer. I found out much later that the beige ones were actually late 50s/early 60s and more desirable than the black ones. I got it from a lad called Tony when Notsensibles were still going. I swapped my *Carlsbro Stingray* for it. He wanted to do a straight swap. No chance. In the end, he gave me forty quid as well.

I remember saying to Tom, 'My rock & roll days are over.' Funnily enough, I didn't have one single enquiry from the ad in the paper, so I ended up keeping the Vox.

The bass was sold to a bloke who was doing a summer season on a cruise ship. A few months later, I went in the music shop and there it was again hanging on the wall. The bloke had sold it back to the shop. I immediately bought it back for a tenner more than I'd sold it for. Fate is weird sometimes – turns out I wasn't giving up rock & roll after all.

11. Emergency 2

Wed 17th June. Table, top of ranch.

Sometimes, when I come up to the ranch, I try and do nothing for a while – just sit and watch. The longer I sit, the more there is to see: birds in the treetops; cars on the roads in and above the town; a building that I've never noticed before; a farm in the far distance; a passing plane; Linda's feral cat creeping by.

My mum used to help with the young naturalists club in the park up the road from our house. Michael and I were dragged along. We thought it was a bit naff. I'd already had a spell at being a twitcher as a member of the *Young Ornithologists' Club*. Roger had an interest in nature too. I remember he had the *Observer's book of fungi*. This was long before we started the band. He ended up working on the parks. I quickly grew out of that early gardening spell, but when I start reading Carlos, I got interested in medicinal plants. All the main characters in the books as well as being *brujos* had also at one time been *yerberos,* i.e. they gathered medicinal plants in the countryside and sold them at markets. Each *yerbero* had their own sales pitch and call – a bit like old-fashioned paper sellers or rag-and-bone men in this country.

There's also a very powerful tradition of plant medicine related to Buddhism and kung fu. The physicians of the Samurai era had the unique position of being able to move freely between all strata of society within feudal Japan – I quite like that idea. There's a saying in Tibetan Buddhism about some monks going into the woods to gather plants then asking the Buddha which of them had medicinal properties. 'All of them', was his reply (I think there's another punch line to the story as well – something like, 'provided you know what to do with them', but I can't remember exactly what it is). I bet that the witch hunts of the 17th century resulted in the loss of a lot of ancient knowledge about plants.

I used to go out walking a lot and I became very interested in identifying the wild plants that I came across. The interest carried on when I got the ranch. When I finally get round to doing a plant sale in the van with my glamourous assistant, I will be giving a nod to the *yerberos.* 'Come on down! Get yer native wild plants! Make your own medicine!' One day maybe.

I got fed up of busking and fancied doing something more interactive and structured. Plants and their uses became a passion and I wondered if there was a way of making a living out of it. I researched all kinds of courses. I thought that a lot of them sounded a bit wishy-washy. I never bought the idea of alternative medicine. Medicine is medicine. To paraphrase a Buddhist proverb, it doesn't matter who removes the poisoned arrow. Alternatively, if you've got a broken hip or appendicitis or if you're in a bad car crash, no amount of 'alternative' medicine is going to help.

At the other end of the spectrum every little niggle is medicalised and there are lots of conditions with acronyms that didn't exist when I started. We are conditioned by the medical establishment and pharmaceutical industries into thinking that we can only use proprietary medicines and that we must go to the doctor's for just about every imaginable ailment. Common sense is no longer common. A plant can't be patented like a drug, so the commercial incentives to research the medicinal properties of a complete plant are different. Questioning everything and making up your own mind is very relevant to healthcare.

As I continued researching, I came across straightforward anatomy and medical sciences and physiology courses. The germ of the idea of doing a medical sciences degree crept into my head. It would provide me with a solid scientific background. My father-in-law was a doctor and I had great admiration for him. What if I could become formally qualified in proper medicine before stepping sideways into plant medicine? What a stupid idea. At my age? With my background? A twat like me? Not a chance. I quickly brushed that twat plan under the carpet and forgot all about it. Too right.

Only I didn't. Or rather I couldn't.

It just wouldn't go away.

It wouldn't leave me alone.

I secretly started researching and looking at medical school prospectuses at the library. I found out that I needed three high-grade A levels. None of my existing engineering qualifications counted for anything. I also found out that most medical schools didn't entertain anyone above a certain age. I was already too old. Forget it.

Late one evening, I had to take a friend to hospital with a hypoglycaemic attack. My first impression was that the nurse who took us in was brusque and downright rude. She called a scrawny little frightened boy who turned out to be the House Officer. He didn't have a fucking clue what to do, so he called the Registrar who arrived about fifteen minutes later looking singularly pissed off. If arrogance could be personified, then he WAS that personification. He was huffing and puffing and exuding a pall of 'What the fuck are you wasting my time with this crap for?' He gave some IV glucose, mumbled something to the nurse and then fucked off again. We got out a few hours later and I couldn't help thinking, 'I'm sure I could do better than that.'

On the day that our daughter was born, I walked into the local college and enrolled for A levels. They told me that I had no chance of getting into medical school, but there were lots of opportunities to work in allied specialities. One of the teachers said, 'Aim for the stars and you might just reach the moon.'

University interviews take place before you sit your A levels. I got a couple of interviews but I had no self-confidence and I didn't have a clue. The only place that I really wanted to go was Manchester. My interview was disastrous and they told me categorically that I would never get a place there. I passed my A levels but I didn't get into medical school. I got a part-time job as a lab technician at another local college which suited me fine.

Louise was pregnant again and all was going well. She was nearly at full term then one awful day, she lost the baby. She had an abruption and bled heavily. It was a grim surreal nightmare of the darkest proportions. We arrived at hospital and a tense crowd of midwives and doctors gathered around. They did an ultrasound and a few moments later a doctor announced loudly to the crowded room:

'Dee baybay ees nort biable.'

Louise's terrified gaze panned round the gathered faces looking for clues. She couldn't understand what he was saying. The doctor repeated the phrase over and over again. He was saying, 'The baby is not viable.' I was the silent witness. I knew what he was saying and had to tell her. I thought, 'Aren't you supposed to be trained in breaking bad news you tactless fuckwit?' He must have skipped that bit.

That was just the beginning. The poor girl had to go through a full labour to deliver the baby. I thought that the midwives were fat and fucking rude. In a calculated act of spectacular cruelty they placed a young student nurse to sit with us throughout the labour. Guess what? The student was pregnant with only a couple of weeks to go. She spent the whole time prattling on about her baby. I was thinking, 'Get this fucking peanut-brained bitch away from us,' but of course I was too polite to say anything. We had very brief contact with the consultants. I found them to be blasé and arrogant.

The baby was perfect. Oh how excruciating and exquisite the sadness when she held him and gave him the gentlest and sweetest of soliloquies. We had to go through the miserable indignity of a funeral for a child that never breathed. We were fucked but carried on. The experience was a catalyst and once again I thought, 'I'm sure I could do better than that.'

I liked working at the college. I made houses for locusts and all kinds of things. I worked part-time and was making enough for us to manage a frugal lifestyle. I was still very much into the idea of growing plants to sell and I had plenty of time to develop the ranch but I somehow knew that there was something else waiting for me. I decided to have another go at getting into medical school. The college was geared up for helping people get into university and they were very kind and helpful. I decided to write to a select number of medical schools saying, 'If I apply to you will I get fair consideration?' No way was I going to write to the posher prestigious ones because I knew I didn't stand a chance.

Pauline, a feisty Scot, was one of the other lab technicians. She'd had a hand in persuading me to re-apply. 'Nonsense,' she said. 'You must write to all of them.'

So I did.

Much to my amazement, I got an encouraging reply from St Andrews, Scotland's most ancient university. The only other encouraging reply I got was from St George's in London. I got a lovely phone call from a very kind doctor. The rest of them wrote back saying, 'Fuck off hippy – no chance.' (Or words to that effect).

I sent in my application form and I got an interview at St Andrews. This time I prepared as well as I possibly could. I had practice interviews with the college and my brother. I anticipated every imaginable question and rehearsed my prepared answers over and over again.

Don Juan talks a lot about 'behaving impeccably'. The day of my interview arrived and for once, every moment was impeccable with minute attention to detail. I wore my old dogtooth check suit that I'd bought over ten years ago in Oxfam and the obligatory Scottie dog cufflinks that Louise bought me. I spent every single moment of the train journey mentally preparing.

I'd booked a B&B in St Andrews. When I arrived, the owner asked me if I was on duty? I don't know what he thought I was? Maybe a CID copper? Just before heading to the interview, I walked right to the end of the pier and balanced on the edge looking out to sea.

They didn't ask me a single question that I hadn't anticipated. At first I was shaking but I got into my stride and I did my best. When I came out I felt good. I couldn't possibly have tried any harder. I couldn't possibly have done any better. St Andrews is a small town with three parallel main streets. After the interview, I was walking along South Street when I noticed a car following me and a bloke waving at me. 'This is weird,' I thought. I looked closer and realised that it was Dr Frame, one of the three who had interviewed me.

'Your wife is cooking sausages and we've decided to offer you a place.' He'd already phoned our house. I went into the first pub and had an ale. My favourite Joy Division song was on the duke box*. 'It's an omen,' I thought.

---

* *No Love Lost* off their 1978 debut *Ideal For Living* EP – I bought it when it first came out and foolishly swapped it Haggis – for what, I can't remember. I also had the 12" version which came out later – both are worth a few bob now.

12. Heading North

Thurs 2nd July. Table, top of ranch.

(You do know how to whistle, don't you Steve?...)

It's been a mixed June with quite a bit of rain but dry for the last couple of weeks. We occasionally get long dry spells up here and when we do, I spend a lot of time watering. I do it all with buckets and watering cans. There's a well at the top that I dug years ago and when things get dry and the water butts are all empty, it's the last supply of water. I dug the well in that spot after divining for it with two bits of sawn-off tent pole and two bits of wire bent at ninety degrees. Divining (also known as dowsing) is an ancient tradition used to find underground water (and lots of other things such as minerals and pipes). There's no scientific evidence to back it up and lots of people brush it off as complete bullshit. I was one of those people. In this country, a forked hazel twig was traditionally used. I did some research and read that you could use two pieces of wire bent at ninety degrees supported in handles made from metal pipe. The idea is that you walk along with the wires pointing forward and as you come upon a water supply or whatever they cross over. I tried it and nothing happened so I wrote it off as nonsense. For some reason, I tried it a second time a few days later. When I wasn't thinking about it, the rods unmistakeably crossed as I walked over a particular area towards the top. When I dug down a foot or so, there was a hefty metal pipe there. It must have been a land drain.

Here's a classic example of something that defies conventional scientific thinking but works. I've always thought that an important aspect of an enquiring mind is to accept that there will always be things that are beyond human understanding.

I have a bucket with a knotted rope that I chuck in the well. There's a knack to it. You have to drop it in upside down. It fills with water then rights itself. Given my engineering background, it's pathetic that I haven't rigged up some kind of irrigation system yet. A solar-powered water pump wouldn't be that difficult to set up.

Redcurrants and raspberries are always the first fruit to ripen. Every year we end up with lots of redcurrant jam because it's not as nice as the blackcurrant, damson, and gooseberry that follows later. It's very seedy. I suppose that's why they make jelly with it. The blackcurrants are ripening now. Louise makes the most exquisite jam. She uses far less sugar than shop-bought. At the height of summer, picking the fruit takes ages. I try and get the fam to help me but they're singularly uninterested. One of my regular tantrums is to point out that their security is dependent on that allotment because it keeps me sane. Their response is one of consistent derision perhaps with a 'fuck off dicktard' thrown in for good measure.

I always feel better for coming up here. When it's sunny like today it's unbeatable. I used to have fruit trees in the centre but I moved everything to the edges to make the most of the light and the view. Today I've got all my jobs done so that I can lounge in the sun trap in front of demi-shed B. It's completely private. Louise is here and we're having an alfresco *répas* with a cheeky vino chilled in the well. She doesn't like the sun and sits in the shade. Chalk and cheese. Who needs Tuscany?

After my St Andrews interview, the summer flew by. At the end of September, we packed our Morris Minor van and headed to St Andrews. Rachel started school and Louise was pregnant again. It was tough going. She'd been ordered to take it easy and I was trying to do the shopping and cooking and look after Rachel. I came back from shopping one day having accidentally reversed into a car in the supermarket car park. The car owner was very understanding. I'd smashed her tail light. We exchanged details and I told her that I'd repair it. I had exams coming up and I was stressed and exhausted. As I was unpacking the shopping, Louise commented that she didn't like 'economy fish fingers'. I snapped.

We had an argument then all of a sudden she was leaking. Oh not again. I'm not religious and I don't believe in god, but in the back of the ambulance I prayed. 'Save the baby and I will do anything.'

They did save him. He was born at Ninewells, the night before my first big exam. It was a wonderful spacious hospital and Louise had her own room overlooking the river Tay. The care was wonderful. I sprinted to Dundee bus station to catch the last bus. The exam was in anatomy. I wanted to beat the Malaysians and come top but I came second by just two marks.

Our tiny baby was in the neonatal unit for ages in a little see-through plastic box with tubes and wires all over him. I bought him a silver *quaich*. Welcome little boy. It was nearly Christmas and The Lord Provost of Dundee came round and gave all the ladies a little commemorative spoon. Louise cried all the time. I couldn't look after Rachel on my own so my dad and Kathleen came and took her back to their house in Ainsdale. It was the Christmas school holidays. She'd only just turned five. It was years later that I realised how frightening and lonely starting school up there had been for her. She never complained and just seemed to take it all in her stride. I was once taking her to school when her little case came open and everything fell out. She just burst into tears.

I watched them drive away. She waved from the back seat looking so tiny and vulnerable – so beautiful with her blonde ringlets. The rest of the day was lost. My heart was broken. I curled up in a ball. Boys Don't Cry – phew. Things would never be the same. When she came back on the train with Louise's sister Lesley a couple of weeks later, there was a screaming baby taking away her mummy's attention.

One morning Eileen from across the road knocked on the door. She had knitted a tiny little suit for the baby. He was doing well. He screamed a lot. He'd spent five weeks in hospital but now he was growing fast. He was soon crawling. There's a wonderful photo of him emptying potatoes out of the kitchen cupboard in our rented house on Doocot Road.

I'm struggling to describe the particular quality of Scotland and the Scots that I love so much. I'm definitely biased. The bottom line is that they were fair (and they saved our baby). They gave me a chance when no-one else would. What is it they have that the English haven't? Perhaps a certain rugged modest majesty; a quiet eloquence; a hint of dourness; a subtle sparkling wit, all forming a tough outer shell that only thinly disguises the most wonderful kindness imaginable. Let's not get too carried away. There are parts of Scotland where an English accent will guarantee you a *Glasgow Kiss.*

St Andrews is a beautiful place. As usual I was too uptight and afraid to make the most of it. I didn't quite fit in with the university toffs and the locals didn't really mix with the students. Right at the end, I met some local musos and started relaxing a bit more. The Dalai Lama came one day and spoke at the university. I went to see him. He was very jolly.

Louise loved it. Fife is a beautiful part of the world with majestic seaside and lots of charity shops. What a combination. There was a wonderful Sunday car boot sale on the old airfield at Cupar.

I was once walking back along the *Laid Braes* late at night when I was accosted by a bunch of drunken locals. I wasn't scared. I think they had the notion of kicking my head in but once they heard my accent and I told them I was from The North, it was fine.

As kids, one of our most memorable holidays was to Girvan. We stayed on a farm. I heard bagpipes for the first time and I secretly wished I was Scottish. My dad used to tell us that we were entitled to wear the McKay tartan because my mum's dad was a Scot. Louise's dad was from Glasgow.

In the 60s, all St Andrews medical students went to Dundee for the second clinical half of their course. When Dundee formed its own medical school, St Andrews needed to find somewhere to send its students. The first pre-clinical half of the St Andrews course is three years instead of the usual two and you end up with a BSc in medical sciences. St Andrews medical school deservedly has a great reputation.

Manchester, a much larger medical school also has a great reputation. St Andrews came to an arrangement with Manchester to take the entire cohort of pre-clinical students (about a hundred or so). The arrangement has worked well ever since. By a serendipitous twist of fate, I ended up going to Manchester after all. Years later, when I was qualified and working at Salford, David Yates, the first professor in Emergency Medicine, asked me to give talks at Manchester medical school to prospective medical students who were taking their A levels.

I was in awe and very nervous of him at first but I soon realised that he was wonderfully supportive and encouraging. He had an old Land Rover. He liked the fact that I came from a different background and he was very keen on encouraging people from different walks of life to apply for medicine.

I would go along and tell my story in front of a lecture theatre packed with A level students, their parents and university bigwigs in bow ties. I can't describe my abject terror when I first did it. The Prof offered subtle criticism and encouragement and after I'd done it a few times, I'd overcome my fear of speaking in public so I have him to thank for that.

When I arrived for my first talk, I was met by the admissions secretary who was most courteous and polite. 'Welcome, Dr Hartley.' She was the same one who had told me years before that there was no possibility that I would ever get into Manchester medical school. She didn't remember me but I remembered her. I didn't say anything.

During my last year at St Andrews, Louise got pregnant again and we decided that she would stay at home close to her mum, and I would go back to St Andrews on my own. As my final exams approached she was at about twenty-six weeks. I phoned up one day and she said that she had the most awful pain in her right side. In an instant I knew that she had appendicitis. I told her to go to hospital. Oh no, not again. I shot down the motorway as fast as I possibly could.

Louise had been admitted to hospital but nothing much was happening. When I arrived, she was sitting there, slightly flushed and not moving. She has a fierce and stoic self-preservation mode and whereas a normal person would be kicking up a fuss, writhing in agony and screaming for painkillers, she said nothing. It's an attitude born of her past experience at the hands of medical professionals so who can blame her?

I did kick up a fuss and I asked to speak to the doctor. A short time later a registrar arrived and I patiently explained to her that Louise had appendicitis which might not be obvious because she doesn't behave like other people.

Her response was sneering, condescending and dismissive. I could see what she was thinking: 'This twat thinks that he knows everything because he's a medical student.' I could read her mind. We'd been here before. You fucking arrogant patronising bitch.

None of them would believe me and we had to wait an agonising further two days for Louise's appendix to rupture and for her to become septic. They finally got round to operating. Fair enough – I can understand their reluctance to operate on a pregnant woman but wouldn't it have been better to get it out before it ruptured? She could have got peritonitis. Afterwards, not surprisingly her uterus began contracting. Fortunately, they managed to stop it and she had an elective caesarean at thirty-six weeks. I never got angry at them. I was too overwhelmed with fear and anxiety.

I can empathise with the agony of families who know that there is something wrong with their loved one and can't get the medical profession to believe them. Let's not be too one-sided – there are scores of medical professionals who are the epitome of professionalism and compassion. It's just that in contrast to Ninewells, we didn't seem to come across that many of them at our local hospital.

I'm sure that was my fate, my lesson. When I finally started working there as a house officer I was more of an arse than any of the ones I'd encountered in the past. Stress does weird things to you and perhaps the hardest part of the job is learning to deal with it. They don't really teach you that at medical school.

Getting through medical school and my junior doctor years with young children was no joke. Now when I look back, it seems inconceivable. I was a grumpy arsehole a lot of the time. Somewhere along the way, I completely forgot my original intention of qualifying then somehow stepping sideways into plant medicine. Before I knew it I was on a roller-coaster. A medical career is tough enough for ordinary sensible people. It's so much harder for a not sensible dick like me who has to do everything the hard way. If things are easy I start thinking that I don't deserve it – imposter syndrome with knobs on and all that.

There are lots of different specialities in medicine. I mentioned earlier that when John Peel died, I wrote a tribute to him and sent it to a magazine who published it. The magazine was *The British Medical Journal* and in the same article I jokingly compared certain medical specialities to different genres of music, the punch line being of course that emergency medicine is the Rock & Roll speciality.

When I was doing my obs and gynae attachment at St Mary's in Manchester in my fourth year of medical school, I had a room right at the top of the building. I could sit on the broad window sill and see right down Oxford Rd towards the centre. We were supposed to assist with a certain number of deliveries. It was tough, because the midwives didn't seem very keen on the medical students – they gave priority to the midwifery students which is understandable I suppose.

One evening, John Peel was standing in for Mark Radcliffe and Marc Riley. He was broadcasting from BBC Manchester just down Oxford Road (before it moved to

Media City). He sounded very homesick and dejected and asked if there was anyone around who fancied going for a pint. It didn't even occur to me to sprint down the road and turn up at the BBC – too shy as usual. I wish I had.

Throughout medical school, I hung onto my love of music and tried to keep playing. On my application form, I didn't dare mention that I'd played in a punk band in case it stood against me. As it turns out, people are very interested when they find out that you've done something a bit different.

In those days, getting into medical school from a different background wasn't easy. It's changed a lot now and mature students have become a lot more fashionable. The majority of medical people are just as ordinary and down-to-earth as anybody else. More importantly, I can report to you that the people (at least in the area of the north of England where I work) who attend emergency departments are by and large thoroughly decent and humble in the face of adversity.

By the way, people who work in emergency medicine refer to it as emergency medicine which takes place in an emergency department. Publicly it's still referred to as A&E. It's highly amusing hearing doctors who don't come near the emergency department using the ancient redundant expression 'casualty'.

Of course in emergency departments you see the disenfranchised and vulnerable along with the whole spectrum of humanity but the disruptive drunks are a relative minority.

I lurched and stumbled along my rocky career path. Why sit one expensive difficult membership exam when you can sit two? My love of Edinburgh is born of my many trips there to fail exams. I coincidentally became a member of the Royal College of Surgeons of Edinburgh and the Royal College of Physicians of Edinburgh in the same month. At that time, the surgeons ran the A&E membership exam but it's all changed now and The Royal College of Emergency Medicine runs its own show. My background became an advantage. I still lived in an ordinary terraced house and I never acquired any middle class aspirations or pretensions (I hope). I got on well with everybody and I never subscribed to any 'us and them' divisions that can sometimes exist in a medical environment.

My greatest heroes will always be nurses. Especially emergency medicine nurses (obviously I'm biased). They work under the most arduous of circumstances and I worry that the intensity of the work is increasing to the extent that the job will become unsustainable over a lifetime's career. As ever, I remained a bolshy gobshite with a healthy disrespect for authority. That gobshittery would come forth when I witnessed bullying – particularly of nurses.

I've always believed that public employees have a special responsibility to act with complete respect and transparency towards the public, in the knowledge that their livelihoods are funded by them and that they are answerable to them in every way. When I see what I perceive to be abuse of a position of authority, I have to speak out. I do have a rather naughty devil's advocate streak, and challenging jobsworths can be rather a fine sport. I've never been one to kiss the hypothetical arse of authority. I always spy the dangling trollocks at the last minute and as I take the institutional bow to make the embrace, my martial arts years somehow spring to mind. I simply can't resist a last minute swirl and kerthwappity-thwap-thwap. How sweet the squelch. I am like the small boy in the fairy story.

'The Emperor isn't wearing any clothes... (and he looks like a dick).'

In the late 2000s a lady started a campaign to investigate Mid-Staffordshire hospital after her mother had died there in the most awful of circumstances. She was patronised and ignored but she persevered and eventually she broke through. There followed a number of investigations and reports leading to intense scrutiny of all aspects of the

NHS. A catalogue of horrific neglect and mistreatment of patients was exposed.

I worked at a hospital that had merged a few years ago with another local hospital twelve miles away. Hospital mergers are happening throughout the UK in a bid to make the most efficient use of NHS resources. Our hospital had never been designed to serve a catchment area of over half a million people and struggled from the outset. The emergency department (and the closely allied medical and surgical assessment units) are the front line of any busy hospital and can quickly become bottle-necked.

We were no different to many other district general hospitals who were struggling to cope with ever-increasing impossible demands. Like many other emergency departments, we were staffed by a disparate bunch of under-resourced consultants. We did our best. Mid-Staffs could just as easily have happened at our place and probably several others.

I remember a world-war two documentary where an American battalion were dug into a hilltop, under constant bombardment by German artillery. It sounds a bit over-dramatic to use a wartime analogy to compare an overwhelmed emergency department to a war zone but I honestly believe that at certain times it's the closest comparison.

As a bunch of consultants, you could say that we were battle-hardened and weary. The front line battle however wasn't the only one. We were subject to the diktats of an ever-changing conveyor belt of managers of various denominations who would randomly announce sweeping changes to the department and the way we ran it without actually bothering to consult us. On almost a daily basis, we would experience various swarms of officials sweeping through our department without bothering to introduce themselves. I affectionately (privately of course) christened them *'cunts with clipboards.'*

My medical soulmate and I trained together and became consultants around the same time. Like me, she's from one of the myriad Northern towns beginning with 'B'. We share a certain ordinariness and we both had a deadpan *laissez-faire* acceptance towards some of the insanity going on around us.

One particular day, I'm worn out and exasperated. I'm weary to my bones of arguing with patronising rude fuckers who know little or nothing about the reality of the emergency department. In my head at least, I have gone off the end of the scale of the politicalincorrectnessometer. One of the biggest problems that we have on a daily basis is referring patients to other specialities. In order to refer a patient, you have to ring the RMO or RSO* or whoever and present the case to them. It's then up to them to 'accept' the patient. It's such an outdated way of doing things. We have more experience than most of them put together, yet we have to expend vast amounts of our energy arguing with them to accept patients.

One junior doctor in particular is driving us mad asking endless unnecessary questions. She then inevitably says, 'Phone me back with the results.' We end up having a word with her consultant. I'm thinking, 'What this waspy bitch needs is...' I would never dare utter such words but then my kindred colleague turns to me with that certain unique eye-rolling exasperated look that she has. She telepathically plucks the words out of my head and says what I'm thinking. I feel much better.

Another day, rather suddenly, we get a new 'management team'. Without any prior discussion, they take over our office and chuck us out. From the word go, there's something deeply unsettling about this 'team'. The needle on my cuntometer is slapping into the red every time I'm around them. I trust my intuition and people confide in me. I begin to hear the most horrendous tales of nepotism and bullying and it's happening right under our noses. After one astonishing episode, I had a rant in our weekly

---

* Receiving Medical Officer, Receiving Surgical Officer.

consultants' meeting. I pointed out that if we didn't speak out against what was going on, we were all complicit. Exposing corruption can be difficult. People are afraid to speak out through fear of reprisal.

Bureaucracy isn't my forte. I found myself being called to numerous meetings and writing myriads of twatty letters (inspiring the song *Letter Writer* on the album). One smarmy manager in particular (who I privately christened *The Avuncular Cunt*), was awash with Melvin-Braggesque mannerisms and at one point told me that I should go and work somewhere else. I knew pretty early on that I hadn't kissed any of the correct arses in the correct manner and that it was only a matter of time before I left.

Doctors and nurses are regulated by very stringent professional bodies (The General Medical Council and The Nursing and Midwifery Council). Managers on the other hand have no regulatory body and often when the shit hits the fan they leave to go to a better job without ever being answerable for their fuck-ups.

One day, an ex-builder was appointed into our midst to work in a crucial role within the department. After a couple of days, my colleague Tom observed that he had the same surname as one of the 'team'. It turns out that he's her husband. What a coincidence. Nepotism or what? We'd had no involvement in the interview process. He would waddle around in builder's arse-crack fashion, trying to interfere in the running of the department. He made snide personal comments and my devil's voice was saying, 'Fuck off and mind your own business. If you can spell 'write' or 'necessary' or 'professional', dicktard thicko, I'll give you a million pounds.' Taff's right – I can be a right arrogant bastard sometimes.

One event that astounded me was the removal of a large television from the main office. The husband and wife carried it out to their car after work one day and took it home 'for safe keeping'. It must have looked like a scene out of a comedy show. When a telly was needed for the new urgent care centre, the one in their possession wasn't mentioned. To me this was a symptom of a pervasive arrogance. Any other institution would regard it as theft.

These people thought that they could do whatever they wanted. I went through the farce of the whistle-blowing process for a good reason of my own. Finally, after a lot of procrastination on the part of the hospital trust, I met with a senior manager who told me that everything had been investigated satisfactorily. No further action would be taken which was pretty much what I expected. The telly 'safe-keepers' kept their jobs. Where I come from, that's called corruption but obviously they didn't agree.

The contempt that this particular senior manager exuded towards me was so thick that you could almost cut it with a knife. He had a CID haircut and a facial expression reminiscent of Rowan Atkinson when he's pissed off with Baldrick. The meeting took place on Christmas Eve and I was buzzing because for the first time in my career I was going to have the whole of Christmas and New Year off with my family. Nothing could taint my relief at getting out of that place and having a long break to enjoy.

My imagination was working overtime as I observed his institutional mannerisms and closed body language. It was a bizarre situation but I didn't say anything – I just kept staring at him.

I recalled the time during one of my many sleepless tortured nights that I'd invented the cunt register and the UCA*. It quickly became apparent that this cunt qualified for both. I was dying to say, 'yes, but the doctor says there's no cure for being a ...'

Suddenly, quite unexpectedly, he delivered the most delicious Christmas gift. His phone went off and guess what? He had a *Bon Jovi* ring tone. I just couldn't have made it up – the cunt with the Bon Jovi ring tone. Oh how very sweet and apt.

I later wrote an instrumental called *Whistleblower* with farting noises and a couple of spoken word lines: '*You do know how to whistle don't you?*' (paraphrasing Lauren Bacall). '*Ou est la television? Ou se trouve la television?*' How very very childish.

In ancient Greece, physicians took *The Hippocratic Oath*. This doesn't really exist today as such but its principles are encompassed in the General Medical Council's *Duties of a Doctor*. My favourite motto that embraces and transcends all of these codes is '*Above all be kind.*' These people were

---

* Ultimate Cunt Award.

working within an institution that should be enshrined in benevolence towards others. I found their rude unkindness and cruelty astounding.

With hindsight, I could perhaps have been less petulant but as my good friend Sandra says, *'To thine own self be true.'* I don't think I would have done things much differently. I'm proud that even under the pressures of their sneaking, lying and bullying, I never flinched once from exposing the truth. They can all fuck off. In fact they did in the end. Every single one of them. *Truth will out,* as they say round here. I'll never know to what extent my arrows of truth contributed to their downfall.

Over a year after I'd gone, a dear friend became very ill shortly after reading an email from a director who was putting her under enormous pressure. To me it seemed like yet another example of the horrendous bullying that went on at that place. It made me very sad and guilty for leaving her behind. I was out. Battered and bruised but in one piece and free to do things on my own terms. Be careful what you wish for. Now I could concentrate on what I really wanted to do. I remembered my original intention of moving into some kind of plant medicine. I had a plan. I didn't want to give up serving humanity. I would work for myself through an agency for a couple of years, then step sideways – grow plants to sell; make guitar amplifiers; finish my record; finish my book. Whoohoo.

13. Field

I'm almost going to Narnia except instead of a wardrobe, it's a corrugated iron gate. Instead of the bleak snowy forest landscape, it's a sunny field. I open the gate and the light pours through into my relatively shaded allotment. The field stretches above reminding me of an Andy Wyeth painting. Long grass is swaying in the breeze and the sun is bright. Even in the shade of the hedge it's hot. I walk to the top and there is the most magical and stunning view over the town with that famous hill in the distance. There are sheep bleating in the surrounding fields and a family of crows are perched in a tall silver birch. Maybe it's not

Narnia. Maybe it's Middle Earth. This time last week, the gate wasn't there. I've just finished making it.

Monty has been my neighbour up here ever since I bought my allotment. He's from southern Ireland. He's a horse man. In fact he's a bit of a horse whisperer on the quiet. He usually has at least two horses. He buys and sells them and breaks them in. He's built a huge stable. We both appreciate the peace and solitude of this place and we both keep ourselves to ourselves. It's no surprise then that it's taken a good ten years for us to start getting to know each other. We're pretty reserved in this part of the world.

Early on, when I'd just got the ranch, the fence between us was in need of repair. I was putting some stuff in a plastic bag one day when one of his horses charged and barged its way in through the damaged fence. Fuck. What am I supposed to do now? I didn't know that the rustling of plastic bags attracts horses. They presume that it's full of carrots just for them. I ignored it and it stomped back into its field. Monty just laughed when I told him. He's full of charming tales about when he first came to England. Like me he was transfixed when he first discovered this hidden quarter beyond the railway bridge. Inevitably he was shunned by the locals. After persevering, he managed to rent an allotment and start keeping horses. He ended up with the big field next to mine. Later, he bought a place a mile up the road. I've been to see it. He's built a wonderful shed with a mezzanine floor and lots of space. He has a small tree plantation and grazing for his horses. He takes them up there every summer.

One day I took him up to the ruins of our old family farm on the moors above the town. It's across the valley from his place. Many years ago, my dad's great grandad had the largest livery stables in town. They used to run out the horses on an area known as *The Red Moss* and they had a small farm close by. Just above the farm is a hillock with traces of a pond at its summit. It commands an awesome panoramic view and I'm convinced that there's something very ancient and special about the place. Once, Ken Spencer, a well-known local historian and a good friend of my mum's gave me a copy of a clipping from an old newspaper – our ancestor, Thomas Hartley, had been fined for burying a horse up there.

I find it amazing that horses remain an integral part of society in this modern day and age. They're expensive to keep and take a lot of dedication so it's a labour of love. Although I'm not a horse person, I come into contact with them via my neighbours. I'm wary of them. I've seen quite a few nasty horse accidents in A&E. I do have some vague equine credentials. Apart from the family livery stables, my mum's dad had been a horse-breaker in the army and my dad's grandad was coachman to Lady O-Hagan at Towneley Hall. The current cafe was originally the stables.

I've observed over the years that people who keep animals in an outdoor setting often have a certain brand of no-nonsense common sense. The intuition that allows them to connect closely with animals and gain their trust maybe gives them an insight into human nature too. They're generally quite private and don't suffer fools. Linda, my other horse neighbour is a perfect example. I see the cat that lives on her allotment regularly. It doesn't go near humans apart from her.

One day, much to my surprise, Monty told me that he was downsizing and selling his field. He said that he'd already given someone else first refusal and if they didn't take it, he wanted me to buy it. He had it valued by an agricultural estate agent. I thought about it and decided that I couldn't afford it and I already had enough to keep on top of. Months went by and none of the other allotment owners had bought it so I made him an offer and he accepted it. My initial feeling whenever I spend a lot on something is one of great anxiety. I had to get a bank loan. I knew that I wouldn't have any trouble because I'm an exemplary customer and I don't do debts. I've never had a credit card and never will. It transpires that because I've never been a slave to their vile blood-sucking financial usury, I actually have the worst ever credit rating. They charged me a staggering 16% interest. How I detest banks and bankers. They rule the world. I've placed them all on the cunt register and issued them all with UCA's.

Given my inherent caution and nervousness, it took a year to sink in that I actually had a one and a half acre field. A wild sloping rugged field trod by horses for over thirty years with a wonderful view of the town and surrounding hills. Everything that I've been rehearsing in microcosm for years could be extended out into smallholding proportions. It finally came home to me when I built that gate between my existing allotment and the field and opened it for the first time to let in the streaming sunlight – a dream come true. I learned more about permaculture and read somewhere that a one-acre smallholding could potentially support five people. Now that's something special. Fortune smiles on the brave.

Being an aspiring smallholder is taking precedence over other pastimes and music is taking a back seat. I'm making a simple record to go with the book – just me and guitar recorded live. As a guitarist, you get weary. You get tired of humping a very heavy amp and you get sick of the noise. More to the point though, you get tinnitus and start going deaf. That's how I came to design and build my own guitar amp. Guitar nerds pay as much attention to their amps as they do their guitars – it's all part of the sound.

My engineering background gave me the knowledge to build cabs and fashion the metalwork for an amplifier chassis. Apart from soldering leads, I had no electronics knowledge but I knew somebody who repaired valve amps. I asked him if he was interested in the idea of doing the electronics side. He wasn't so I did it myself.

I bought a few books and studied and studied then studied some more. My favourite book by far on old guitar amplifiers is Gerald Weber's *A Desktop Reference of Hip Vintage Guitar Amps*. It's mainly about the late 50s, early 60s Fender designs and that's pretty much all you need. Jim Marshall cloned a *59 Bassman* for his first *Bluesbreaker* amp. The great thing about the book is that it has both diagrams of the components and where they go along with the actual electronics circuit diagram. You can study both side by side and slowly learn about the electronics.

I took all the best qualities of the amps that I've used all my life then added a few of my own. I wanted an amp that would be more portable and robust than some of my old 60s ones. Unlike most modern guitar amps, I wanted it to have two separate channels so that one could be used for vocals at rehearsals and small gigs. I paid minute attention to detail. The lads and I have used it for every gig, rehearsal and recording session since. It attracts attention wherever we play and a few people have asked us about building them one. It's twenty watts and keeps up with the loudest drummer but is relatively light and portable for a valve amp. Most importantly it has the most exquisite perfect valve tone. Sam thinks we should build a few and lend them to local studios and musicians – a possible business for the future?

One-off hand-built guitar amps are often referred to as *boutique* amps for some reason. Dread the thought. Ours are as tough and robust as imaginably possible: eight metal corners; metal grilles; covered in tough furnishing fabric; three coats of floor varnish. They're designed to be Rock & Roll amps for life – hand-wired, simple and infinitely repairable. They're meant to survive having a pint poured on them and being kicked downstairs – perfect for teenagers. It's all part of that neat and tidy concise Rock & Roll ethic.

The Three Platitudes split after I'd been away at medical school for a year or so. I felt like I had too much on at the time. Even though fate had decreed that I would keep my Vox AC30 and Stu Sutcliffe bass, playing music felt like a thing of the past. The seven-day stints of twelve-hour nights soon began and it became a battle with exhaustion and a game of survival. Herein lies the eternal work-life balance conundrum. You need a job to support your family. The job fucks you so much that you make your family life a misery. Finding a middle way is the most difficult of balancing acts.

It took a while for it to dawn on me that music was actually more valuable than ever. Having something outside of medicine that makes your heart sing is desperately important. Also the soothing balm of being outside on the ranch became a lifesaver. Many times, I would rush home from work and get up here as quickly as I could, hoping that I wouldn't bump into anyone on the way. The relief and sense of peace when I shut the door behind me was enormous.

I did get back into playing again and the next manifestation of the puritan 3-piece was with my brother on drums and Michael Spencer on bass. My brother is a brilliant drummer. We'd already played together in a few bands. Michael Spencer is an all-round accomplished musician although first and foremost a guitarist. We decided to form a Rockabilly/Rock & Roll band to play pub gigs.

After lots of debate, we settled on the name *Vincent* (as in Gene Vincent, even though we only did one Gene Vincent song). Michael's a great singer and front man and we got lots of gigs. We were pretty accomplished. We split when Michael emigrated to Australia.

My brother, also an accomplished all-rounder, got a double bass when Michael left and learned to play it. Now we needed a drummer. One day, Louise and I were going up the supermarket escalator and Bish's Joanne was coming down on the other side. 'How's Bish?' I said. 'Oh, he's cleaning his drum kit. He's bored.'

I'd known Bish for years. He plays with *Walter Mitty's Head*. They're a Rock & Roll band with a psychobilly punk edge. They've been going for ages and formed from a couple of post-punk bands. Bish is tall and athletic with a wickedly droll sense of humour. Like me he got his nick-name at school. He was good at cricket and someone said he played like the Indian cricketer *Bishan Bedi*.

At that time he wasn't playing with Walter Mitty's Head and was looking for another band. That was that; Bish joined and we've been playing together ever since. I changed the band name to *Vincent Black Lightning*. I wanted something with a rock & roll ring to it that still had a connection to Vincent. Also it was the name of an English motorbike. *Black Rebel Motorcycle Club* were big at the time and that clinched it. Naively, I was unaware of Richard Thomson's song of the same name until Ollie, my anaesthetist friend at work played it to me. I met Ollie when I was doing my anaesthetic training shortly after my disastrous GP year. I was at a low ebb and one day I dropped a 20ml vial of propofol in the anaesthetic room. I wanted the earth to swallow me up.

We wheeled the patient into the operating room and there was a tense silence. It was a two-hour operation and I couldn't think of anything to say. I happened to mention that I played in two bands and Ollie's face immediately lit up – it turns out he's a full-blown muso. He has a record player and a drum kit and plays guitar. We talked about favourite bands, favourite guitarist, favourite guitar solo and so on. When I told him the band name, he found the song on his iPod and played it for me. It's a wonderful ballad and the guitar playing is magnificent. The hairs on my arms stood on end. If I'd known about that song, I'd have chosen a different name. Ollie has his own band now.

Over a four-year period, VBL recorded a sprawling anthology of 32 songs on the eight-track in the back room. We put them out as an EP, two albums and a 7" single. My brother moved on and Karl Eden joined us on bass. I knew Karl Eden through his band tRANSELEMENt. They'd done three Peel sessions and I'd released a two-part EP *Songs about Travel* for them on my label. The woodblock for the cover depicts a rat with its body on the front of part 1 and the tail on part 2. Typically, Bish and I would record the guitar and drums live, then Karl, a brilliant bassist, would come on a Wednesday and record his bass part. He played most of the bass lines on the records. One of my favourite recordings is *Baa Baa Rainbow Sheep* which is an observation of political correctness gone mad. It's the only track on the records which is completely live. We just played it over and over again until we got it right. It's the first track that I played my beautiful *Gretsch* on.

Bish has the most deadpan sense of humour which is difficult to describe. It's expressionless and doesn't even look like humour to a casual observer. One of the best examples was when we played at The Crescent in Salford with a band whose name I forget. There was a lady drummer who played an electronic drum kit with fluorescent purple drum sticks that lit up in the dark and a younger lady who played keyboards and sang.

The band was sound-checking and the drummer was messing with the PA. Bish sauntered across the floor, got up on stage, picked up the purple drum sticks and proceeded to play for the sound check. All he did was sit there with an expressionless face and the odd subtle movement. Lee (who played bass with us at the time) and I laughed, then laughed some more – it was one of those torrential 'less is more' comedy moments. In fact we couldn't stop. Lee had to evacuate to the toilets and later he said that he had to get out because his eyelids were turning inside out. Lee's daughter Faron is in a couple of the John Lee Hartley videos and she recorded four songs for an EP that we put out.

When the band took to stage, the same irreverent humour attacked us and we had to move outdoors to avoid appearing rude. I think there was an element of political incorrectness on our part. We can't be PC all the time – we're a Rock & Roll band FFS.

There have been many such moments of comedy. We played at Bingley festival of Original Music (BOMFEST) and were camped in the van in the artistes' enclosure, which had its own blue portable festival toilet. The doors of the van looked directly towards the toilet and as someone went in it, Bish shouted, 'No solids!' It's that Northern sense of humour. Not everyone gets it.

Playing in bands is like a pendulum – you get sick of the gear-humping, late nights, the same old songs and the argy-bargy, but when you stop doing it, you miss it. I decided a while ago that if and when VBL fizzled out, I'd go my own way. Keeping a band together seems to get harder as you get older.

I was going to be plain old Stephen Hartley, but then one day, Sam and I were having a conversation about band names and I mentioned that I wished I'd called him John Lee Hartley (instead of Samuel Edmund John). The name makes me smile – there's the obvious John Lee Hooker similarity and it has a certain rock & roll ring to it. My middle name is John, so I thought I'd keep John Lee Hartley for my music name. It's not the same leap as *Reg Dwight* or *Harry Roger Webb* but it will do. It's also a tribute to my dad. He always used to say that we should name one of our children John. It would have been unfair to name Rachel John, so it had to be there somewhere in Sam's name.

We left registering Sam's birth until the last moment and we still hadn't finalised his name. When we got to the registrar's, we were told that there would be a bit of a wait. Louise nipped off to do a bit of shopping. As soon as she'd gone, the registrar called me in. I went for Samuel Edmond John. I liked Sam, Louise liked Edmond and obviously the tribute to Cowboy John had to be in there. Just as the registrar was completing the last swirl of her copperplate hand writing, Louise burst in.

'What have you called him?'
'Samuel Edmond John.'
'I don't like that.'
'Tough.'

I got a right bollocking because I'd used the wrong spelling of Edmond – it should have been Edmund.

I remember thinking one day, I would love to be involved in film-making – it looks fascinating. I then realised that I already was. I've been making simple little videos to accompany songs for yonks now. I have a couple of film-maker friends and as with everything these days, you can learn all about it on the internet.

I learned that there's a fairly cheap SLR camera that has a good reputation for making videos (Canon 550D) so I bought one off the internet. I bought a 'prime' lens and my video making moved up a whole notch. We've already made quite a few daft John Lee Hartley videos; Bish's comedy genius comes into its own. We record the music first then do all the filming afterwards. Perhaps our best video to date is *Park Keeper* which is inspired by a true-life incident.

The park keepers where we live (they call themselves rangers) have a portfolio of duties that allow them to issue parking tickets and dog shit penalties. They hide in the bushes and spy on dog walkers through binoculars. Along with traffic wardens and wheel clampers to me they represent the lowest form of jobsworth quasi-official, and get right on my tits. As public employees, they are fair game for a bit of sport.

I must admit there's a bit of a throwback from my childhood when loads of us hung around Scott Park. We used to have lots of fun taunting the parkies until they chased us. We were about nine or ten. On one occasion, they planned a sting and closed in on us unexpectedly with three of their dark blue vans. They screeched up in front of us then gave chase on foot. We scattered and I ran down Pendlehurst Street with one of them hot on my heels. I darted left into John Griffiths' back yard and into his coal shed. Luckily for me his dad came out of his back door at precisely that moment. He bellowed at the parky, 'How dare you come running into my property like that?! Get out immediately!' The parky tried to get a word in but he was no match for Arthur Griffiths. I cowered in the shed for a good half hour before I dared skulk off home. We knew all the gardens of all the houses on the surrounding streets. It was our territory. We used to play 'tracking' which was essentially an extended form of hide-and-seek in people's back gardens. Childhood was so much different in those days. We were like feral animals.

Back to the present and my naughty schoolboy streak is as healthy as ever. One day I caught a parky giving out a load of parking tickets to several cars that appeared to me to be legitimately parked. I took him to task. He came out with the inevitable, 'I'm only doing my job,' and I took great delight in a rapier diatribe, pointing out that hiding behind his job didn't absolve him from the consequences of his actions. I asked him how he felt about the misery that he was causing to ordinary folk on their way to a football match. He didn't like it one bit.

A few months later, there was a Sunday derby match on and I spotted the same parky giving a ticket to a car at the bottom of our street. He was taking photos of it. Quick as a flash, I ran out with my camera and crept up behind him and started filming. It took him a while to notice me and when he did, he practically jumped out of his skin.

'You can't film me!'

'Oh yes I can. You're a public servant and it's perfectly legal – what's the difference between me filming you and you taking photos of peoples' property?'

He became very agitated, particularly when I said that this would make a great little *YouTube* video which I would share on *Facebook*. He got his phone out and I thought he was phoning the police but he was phoning his superior.

A couple of days later to my utter disbelief they posted a letter through my door. It was full of typos and spelling mistakes and could have been written by a child. It had a Lancashire constabulary logo at the bottom. It was trying to be very official and threatening but failed miserably due to the bumpkin English and grammar. It was clearly a contrived letter trying to intimidate me. They could have easily lost their jobs if I'd reported them but I didn't want to cause them any harm. I thought it was hilarious and I entered into the spirit of it. After doing quite a bit of research about the local council's disciplinary procedures and finding out the names of the senior parkies, I crafted my reply and it was a masterpiece. My years of experience of writing twat letters came in handy and I had great fun.

In the kindest possible way, between the lines, I was saying '...trespass on my property in order to intimidate me and...' I think they got the message.

The whole experience was quite inspiring and inevitably it spawned a song: 'Park Keeper'. It's a rambling semi-rap which tells the entire tale in full along with a bit of dramatic artistic licence. I came up with a riff inspired by John Lee Hooker's *I'm Leaving*. I play my beautiful 1964 *Hofner Club* on it. Rockabilly Dave played double bass. Making the video was great fun. We filmed some scenes on the field. Bish plays the park keeper and his acting is brilliant from start to finish. Jet stars in it too; there's a scene of him crouching in crapping mode and a couple of chase scenes.

Bish's son Bryn now has a band called the *Goa Express*. We released a single for them and made a video to go with it. Apart from the mastering, the actual pressing and some of the filming, we did literally everything in the back room. We spent ages cutting, folding, gluing and printing the covers. We used bright yellow card. We spent hours and hours filming and editing the video. We managed to get it released as an *Official Record Store Day* record. The band played in Neil's record shop on the day and we sold about fifty singles.

We're very lucky to have two independent record shops opposite each other. Neil's is a goldmine where you can still get class vinyl at reasonable prices without having to use the internet. Lez's across the road still has its original

60s décor complete with listening booths. They filmed some scenes in it for a Northern Soul film.

After Goa had played, Bish, Taff, WA KA and I were standing outside the record shop chatting. It struck me as being quite cool that four blokes with grown-up kids still had their schoolboy nicknames. WA KA is also a pure-bred muso. He puts on bands at The Trades and at the wonderful Golden Lion in Tod with Gig. Gig is an energetic upbeat catalyst, supporting and encouraging art and music. She's done a lot for Tod.

In the evening, we'd organised a gig at The Town Mouse. I happen to glance down when I was carrying in the gear and I noticed *The Salford Arms* in wonderful mosaic tiling in the entrance. It must have been the pub's original name. I keep getting weird little omens about Salford. I'm suspicious of the place. Ever since I worked there as a senior house officer there's been a bizarre connection – it's quite unsettling.

Notensibles' biggest fan Nighty is from Salford. He has our name tattooed on his leg with a section of the album cover as background. He came to my house when we played in the front room once.

The beauty of releasing a 7" single is that it's a neat little self-contained project which isn't too time-consuming. I

like the notion of marrying the old with the new –
obsolete craftsmanship with modern technology.

Bryn is a bit younger than my lads. He's a natural
musician. He first played bass with me and Bish when he
was thirteen and he's in all the John Lee Hartley videos.
From my lads' early teenage-hood, our house was a hive of
social and musical activity. When they first started getting
interested in music, I was vaguely surprised. 'Where the
apple falleth', said Zina nonchalantly when I mentioned it
one day at work. There were a spattering of teenage bands
about and my two started doing odd bits with their friends.
When Elias was fifteen he suddenly said,

'I want a drum kit.'
'But we've already got a perfectly good drum kit.'
'Yours is shit; I want my own; I want a red one.'

Off we went to Reidy's and bought one.

I've been using the same little drum kit for rehearsals and
recordings for years now. It's permanently set up in the
corner of the back room. It's actually a child's drum kit
that I bought from Dawson's music shop when it was
shutting down. Bish has augmented it with a rack tom and
decent cymbals and he's put on new skins and has rebuilt
the snare drum.

After a while, my lads inevitably formed a band. They'd been suffused with my record collection since birth so thank goodness they had a decent taste in music. It was a two-way thing. They would also show me videos of new bands. The Arctic Monkeys were a big part of the backdrop during those years. Sam played guitar, wrote the songs and sang and Elias moved onto bass. They teamed up with Matt and Tyler. Tyler was already legendary as a great drummer. They called themselves *The Strange*. Sam and Tyler were fifteen and Matt and Elias were sixteen. Before that, they briefly had a band called *The Norms,* which I thought was a great name.

So began a tumultuous few rock and roll years. It wasn't particularly sweet and pretty in the way that perfect dads help out with their teenage sons' band. I didn't want to be a roadie and a taxi driver and I had no interest in being their manager. One the one hand it was, 'Fuck off and mind your own business,' and on the other hand it was, 'Er, we have a gig tomorrow – can we have a lift?'

We had many trips in the old magic bus: gigs; rehearsals; recording sessions; festivals; holidays. Often we'd be carrying the band, a couple of mates and all the gear. The lads' bedroom upstairs was party central with a close circle of mates round at the weekends. We were like an extended family. Once a year we rented a nice flat or house somewhere and all went on holiday together.

We recorded a 7" single in the back room. They wanted to go to a 'proper' studio but I wanted them to have a memento for the future. I wanted them to be able to look back and remember that for a brief time they lived in a house that was at the centre of a neat and tidy little Rock & Roll scene. It was the time that Notsensibles were back together and VBL were still going – that meant three rehearsals a week with three different bands in the back room of a scruffy Victorian terraced house in The North of England. Neat. All they had to do was roll out of their slob bedroom and wander downstairs. I built another amp and Sam used one and Matt the other.

One of their early gigs was at The Academy in Manchester – it was in the little venue upstairs. They'd organised it themselves and got a coach with all their mates – so reminiscent of the early Notsensibles days. By coincidence, the *Jim Jones Review* were playing downstairs and Louise and I and a few mates had tickets. We got a minibus. I helped The Strange set their stuff up and watched them briefly from the back. There was a spine-tingling moment when I realised that they had suddenly found their stride and that there was something special there. They did quite a few gigs and there was a real buzz at one time. I captured a lot of it on film.

My favourite is an early Radio session when they played *Weave and Wind*. The band fizzled out a bit when Tyler and

Matt moved to London but we still keep in touch and there's still the occasional gig. Tyler, Bryn and I are nominally *The Jazz Bastards* based on yet another of my daft ideas which is to pretend to be an accomplished jazz band then just get up and fuck about. We've even played live once albeit briefly.

One day, Patti Smith came to town. She played at The Mechanics. Such famous people don't normally come here. She came because she and her sister are very interested in The Pendle witches. She played in Haworth too. I'm not a fan but I thought it was worth getting tickets because she was an important part of the New York punk scene. A few friends went and I got tickets for me, Louise, Elias and Sam. It sold out quickly. On arrival, Elias demanded a pint and a double whiskey chaser. He stuck about ten minutes of the concert then got up and left noisily, muttering derogatory comments: 'This is fucking shit. Fucking hippies.' There was visible shock on the faces of the politely seated middle-aged, middle class hippies. I was quite proud of him.

Due to the ability to print the record labels with my Adana, I like to do a few spoof copies of the singles I release. For the VBL single it was *The Deke Bevington Eclipse* (and another too vernacular to mention) and for The Strange it was *Ichibard Crane and The Mundanes*. I made up spoof biographies to go with them. The Strange also recorded sixteen songs for an album in the back room but never finished them. Tyler is the loudest drummer I've ever heard so it was technically challenging. We recorded the drums over two days and only got a complaint from our fantastic neighbours at the end of the second day.

NOTSENSIBLES had a surprising resurrection. Someone suggested a twenty-five-year reunion of The Railway Workers. We formed a committee and the whole thing was pretty well organised. We had regular meetings and there was a huge buzz. Boff sorted a little fold-out brochure as a keepsake and I printed the tickets on my Adana. I copied an original ticket that Spider had printed back in the day.

One evening the five of us were suddenly back together after a long absence. Gary was living in Salford and Kev tracked him down. We met at my house to rehearse. The first time we struck up playing was a wonderful skin-tingling moment.

On the night of the reunion, the venue was packed; the whole evening was an enormous success. Khany and AnnaMarie came over from Florida. Someone else flew all the way from California to see us. *Tiger Tails* and *Chimp Eats Banana* played. We had a great party at Spider's afterwards.

Spurred by the interest, we carried on, doing the odd gig here and there. My favourite was at the Trades club with

The Strange supporting. We weren't particularly going anywhere but then Margaret Thatcher died and we got in the charts.

That's right, we got in the charts.

Someone had planned an internet campaign to get *Ding Dong The Witch is Dead* to number one. The Tories didn't like it one little bit, so they searched for a song that they could use to rival it and they chose I'm in Love with Margaret Thatcher! You couldn't make it up. They didn't realise that it was a piss-take! We were in all the papers and went on telly twice. Of course, our usual auto-self-destruct soon came into play, but it was great fun while it lasted.

We carried on for a while and eventually split amicably. For me, punk was about youth and rebellion and as ever, the cabaret aspect didn't appeal to me. I wanted to write new songs and be a bit more like Wire and Gang of Four rather than trawl the old punks' circuit. We're all still in touch and still do the odd bit occasionally. I remember a few years ago having a conversation with Boff about continuing to play in a band after the initial youthful splurge has long since gone. Electric Chumawamba had split, and they were playing acoustically, concentrating more on the folky side. Boff said 'There comes a time when you're too old to be jumping up in the air doing scissor kicks.' I immediately thought 'Well I'm not that old yet.' Thereafter I made a point of doing a scissor kick at every Notsensibles gig (even though I did fall over backwards once).

It's business as usual in the back room. Bish and I are using the same compact 8-track set-up that we've used for years. The room has its unique sound. Whereas once we used to use up to 8 mics for a recording session, we now use only two or three – no frills – less is more. We rehearse on Fridays and put out the odd record here and there and make daft videos. Our next project is to do a video of *Up The Ladder and Down Again*. Bish has had the idea to plant a ladder in the field, then film people climbing up and down it dressed in daft costumes.

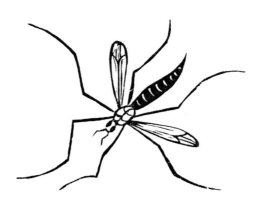

14. America

Tue 28th July. Table, top of ranch.

I get a sudden flashback and I'm in the Record Exchange on Standish St. I'm about fourteen.

I'm flicking through the singles and I pick up a Muddy Waters 7" on Chess. It has a white label and it's called *I'm your Doctor*. It has no middle. I know hardly anything about music but I do know that singles without middles have been played on jukeboxes and are probably knackered. It's only 50p so I buy it anyway.

Meanwhile, like everyone else, I'm absorbing the entire Stones and Beatles back catalogue. I'm starting to pick out the odd record for myself. I get *RHYTHM & ROCK – The best of Chess, Checker, Cadet*. I kind of like most of it, but three tracks grab me and stay with me forever: Eddie Fontaine's

Nothin Shakin – oh what a wonderful rock & roll/rockabilly tune – fantastic guitar playing. The Beatles covered it in their early days and thank goodness there's a recording of it on *Live at The Star Club Hamburg*. It must have seeped into our teenage collective consciousness because Chimp Eats Banana did a great instrumental version. I got a 7" copy of the original on *London* many years later.

Then there's *Wang Dang Doodle* by Koko Taylor and I adore it. The guitar playing is superb and a wonderful chugging guitar riff keeps it going. Koko's soaring vocals are ace. I already mentioned the steamy lyrics. At that age, I didn't have the nous to pick up on them.

Tommy Tucker's *High Heel Sneakers* opens with a memorable guitar riff then breaks into a magnificent shuffling R&B classic driven by Tucker's gravelly voice.

'Put on your high-heel sneakers, we're going out tonight.'

I still don't know what high-heeled sneakers are. I spent hours trying to learn that guitar part. Bo Diddley's *Mumblin Guitar* is great too.

All these recordings have great guitar playing, sparse accompaniment and raw gutsy live recording. That's always been my favourite kind of music and of course it all originated in America. The entire Stones and Beatles repertoire was American Rock & Roll and R&B until they started writing their own songs.

The reason I'm able to hear those records is that enterprising businessmen started labels such as Chess, Stax and Sun. Many of the artists (mostly black) got very little of the profit and invariably their royalty rights were stolen. Still, hopefully their lives improved as a result of getting their music out there.

Even that nasty punk rock music originated in America from the seventies CBGB's scene in New York. It all came from that vast country of contrast. Home of Rock & Roll and Rhythm and blues and also the home of monstrous military might. Three of the songs on the *Vincent Black Lightning* records refer to America's warmongering.

I liked reading about bands on tour in America and a lot of American film and TV inspired my small-time imagination. Still, I had no desire to go there. As a teenager, I barely had the initiative to put my underpants on the right way round in the morning let alone go any further than Manchester on the bus. I think I probably had a vague notion of the segregation that had gone on over there. I'd heard of Martin Luther King.

Back in the UK in the 60s, the first waves of Pakistani immigrants were arriving. Everyone called them *Pakis* but not my mum and dad. My dad taught at *Blakey Moor* school and he had great admiration for the Pakistani children. He taught some of the very first arrivals and said that they were polite and hard-working and very keen to learn. He even learnt some Urdu.

I suppose that racism is the natural default in any parochial small town – certainly much more then that today. Even though segregation in America was quashed years ago, just like everywhere else, covert and more recently, overt racism still exists. When my brother and I were kids, it was different for a couple of reasons.

My mum had a difficult life and didn't have the opportunity to make friends easily. One day, she met a lady at the bus stop and they got on like a house on fire. The lady had children our age and our families became friends. For years we went on camping holidays together. Her husband was from Goa; it just so happened that their children were the only brown ones at our junior school and they were our friends. The notion of racism didn't really enter our heads as small children, but looking back, we didn't have the power of reasoning to pick up on what was going on. In secondary school there were just a handful of Asian kids and my friend Khany happened to be one of them. Fortunately he was as hard as fuck and if anyone was overtly racist towards him he just kicked the shit out of them. His family came to England in 1969 in a

Morris Minor. At first he was bullied. His dad told him to hit back harder so he did. He soon learned to stick up for himself. He and his family moved to America when I was twenty. It was a sad moment. It happened quite quickly. He was a huge part of our teenage lives. He was in Chimp Eats Banana and he livened up things no end with his outlandish humour. He got a pair of the most outrageous kitsch multi-coloured platforms that you could imagine from his dad's shoe shop.

When we all started driving, he used to race round in his mum's car at terrifying speed. He restored an Austin Healey frog-eyed Sprite; he sprayed it a wonderful metallic red. He still has the same outlandish offbeat sense of humour. He and I got into trouble at school once for a series of lunchtime pranks which would probably have us in prison in this politically correct day and age. I still have the letter from the head master to my mum and dad. It's like the kind of thing you would see in *Viz*. After he moved, we kept in touch by letter. There was no internet and mobile phones didn't exist.

I didn't have a clue about anything – my childhood gave me no preparation for the real world. My mum was ill a lot then she died when I was twenty four. That played a big part in my not growing up even though it took me about twenty years to realise it.

Shortly after he left, Khany invited us over to stay with him and Inger got very excited. To me, going to America was an incomprehensible impossibility but Inger persisted and she did all the organising. She had great common sense and insight – enough for both of us. Unfortunately Notsensibles got offered a gig during the time when we were due to be away. It was for our friend Carole Edmundson's eighteenth birthday and they decided to do it without me. Gary played guitar. I was gutted. It was a big garden party with a marquee. Carole was cool. She drove round in her mum's Mercedes.

The day finally came. We both had two weeks off work. There were no direct flights to Orlando in those days, so we had to change at Miami. I remember sprinting through the airport to catch our connection. It was night-time when we got off the plane in Orlando and the first thing that I noticed was the waft off hot air that hit us from the tarmac and a peculiar subtle pervasive smell unique to Florida. We had a wonderful fortnight. Khany had contacts and we got into *Busch Gardens* by climbing over a back fence. We spent a lot of time hanging about with Robert, one of his cool friends from New York.

Khany's family lived in a wonderful house on a lake shore. He drove a green 1970 Buick Riviera. The weather was hot and humid and it often rained in the evenings. I was surprised by how fat a lot of the people were and there were no pavements. It was very much a takeaway culture. I loved *Taco-Tico*. We saw an awful Sex Pistols covers band in a club. We went in some great record shops and I still have a handful of records that I bought there. I learned for the first time that all American singles are pressed without middles so my Muddy Waters wasn't a jukebox record after all. Chess labels are blue but mine was white. That's because it's an advance promo copy for DJs. I still have it and it's actually a bit of a mod classic. I like it because of the title. There are lots of musicians who refer to themselves as various kinds of doctors and lots of bands have at least one doctor song – *Doctor Robert* by the Beatles to name but one. I must be the genuine Rock & Roll doctor then. How many A&E doctors have done a Peel session? I should add it to the CV.

Now I have a field. It's a scrubby sloping field and the land isn't particularly good. It's peppered with dock plants and there's a huge ramshackle stable in the centre. There's lots of broken glass under the surface presumably from previous allotments. An old map from the 1940s shows the area as 'allotment gardens'. It was also part of a farm at one time and would have been meadow land. I'm pleased with it. Most days when I'm up there, I walk round the outside checking on the hedge and the trees and taking in the magnificent view. Today I've picked blackcurrants and rhubarb and harvested a sack-load of potatoes. I've grown a big patch of borage and I've been trying to collect the seed on fleece spread out on the ground but something is eating them as they fall.

I like to watch internet videos on gardening, smallholding, self-sufficiency etc. There are hundreds out there and lots of them are American. I might be wrong, but as far as I'm aware the concept of allotments doesn't exist in America in the same way that it does in this country.

Allotments have been around for centuries. At one time town councils had a legal duty to provide them for the local population (beginning with the 1908 smallholdings and allotments act). During wartime and times of recession, they have been an important national food source. Sadly, as greed and short-sightedness prevails more and more allotment land is seized for building for profit. In some parts of the country, particularly London, the waiting list for council allotments stretches to decades.

Americans have the concept of 'homesteading'. This stems from the 1862 *Homesteading Act* which, for a small registration fee provided 160 acres of land to families. If they developed the land and lived off it continuously for five years, they were granted ownership. The act was officially abolished in 1976 (and unofficially much earlier). Latterly the term refers to living self-sufficiently off the land. It incorporates the use of modern technology such as sun and wind power to live 'off-grid'. Typically American homesteaders are using much more land than I have, but the principles and ideas are the same. It's not just America, it's a worldwide phenomenon and of course it's the way people lived anyway until relatively recently.

The pioneering days of the Wild West grabbed my dad's romantic imagination. He WAS a cowboy trapped in the body of a Northern working class bloke. He even applied to emigrate to Australia once with the dream of working on a cattle farm as a cowboy. He almost went, but decided against after his mum died and his dad was on his own.

He adored watching Westerns on the telly and he would often have one of our cap guns in hand, firing it at the telly. If my dad was a cowboy, then I was an Indian. I was utterly fascinated by the native tribes of a vast country that was certainly never known as America by them before the settlers came and decimated them.

Soon after I'd met Louise, I called round at her house and she and her mum and dad were all avidly watching *Top Gun*. The gist of the film as I remember was the acquisition of the coveted US Air Force pilot's wings. After the film had finished, Louise's dad casually remarked 'I've got one of those.' (meaning the wings badge). He went upstairs and came back with an American US Navy Aviator's wings badge and it was his. He was in The Fleet Air Arm towards the end of the Second World War. He was trained by the American Air Force in the pacific and flew Corsairs off aircraft carriers. He described the exhilaration of taking off and the massive thrust developed by the engine. There's a beautiful photo of him sitting in the cockpit of one. He looks so young and handsome.

Fast forward and I'm waiting to get on the Roosevelt Island Tramway down to the lower East side of Manhattan. There's me, Khany, his daughter Sophia, Elias and Sam. There's a bunch of ultra-cool New York hipsters waiting too. We quietly take the piss and Khany secretly takes a pic and puts it on *Facebook* with one of his characteristically hilarious quips.

It's all Boff's fault – him and his American family and friends. He met Casey, an American girl when he was touring America. Last year in July they celebrated their 20th anniversary at Pete's farm in Wales. Pete was a contemporary of our manager Simon. They both worked at Mid-Pennine Arts Association at the same time back in the day. Pete moved to Wales and bought a ten-acre run down farm on the banks of the river Vyrnwy. He's slowly restored it and built a bunch of charming buildings for people to stay in. He grows hay in his fields for local farmers. People go there for parties and weddings.

It was a thrilling inspiring perfect weekend and I was excited for weeks before it happened. Khany and his family were coming over.

It began on the Thursday afternoon. The weather was deliciously hot, hot, hot with baking sunshine and mild breezes. Khany, Sophia and Boff came to my house. Us lads rehearsed and Louise, Rachel and Sophia walked up the park with Jet. We were getting together a rock and roll set to play on the Saturday afternoon. In his parallel life in America, Khany, like me has continued to play in bands – mainly rock & roll and rockabilly. He plays double-bass (which the Americans call upright bass) and drums.

I was up early the morning after in feverish anticipation. I'd already got the van prepared in full glamping mode. I loaded up my guitar and double bass, and I was off. The journey to Wales was smooth and uneventful and the van ran beautifully. Khany, Sophia and Boff had driven there straight from my house.

As I arrived, Khany was just surfacing from his cabin. He drove the van round the field. We hung out for the rest of the weekend. The weather got even hotter. It felt incredibly glamourous being amongst so many cool arty Americans. Casey's niece Emma and her partner Crusher were there. Crusher is the best double bass player I've heard in my life (and Khany's great too). I was awestruck. He's from New Jersey and regularly frequented CBGB's as a teenager. Emma is an actor and made me laugh by referring to washing up liquid as 'dish soap'. I discovered lots of subtle Americanisms.

Boff and Casey had planned the weekend as their 'wild rumpus' and a right rumpus it was too. On the Friday night we danced till 4am to great DJs, fortified by a free bar. Saturday began in a leisurely fashion with rehearsals in Khany's cabin. Crusher played along to some of my songs and picked them up immediately. In contrast to the complete indifference that greets me in my local environs, he was most encouraging and it was a true breath of fresh air – an inspiration.

In fact that was the crux of the whole weekend – a collective joy and inspiration, celebrating our good fortune and determining to follow our dreams wholeheartedly.

Emma summed it up by saying 'I'm going to keep this weekend on a folded up piece of paper in my pocket.' There was a quality that the Americans had, that us stodgy Northerners don't have – an acceptance and encouraging viewpoint and a quiet confidence that arty stuff is worth pursuing.

Finish that book.
Make that record.
Believe in that acting career.

The afternoon started with a pie-eating contest followed by a tug-of-war – UK versus America. Guess who won? Pete has made an avenue of arched willow bordering one of his fields and perhaps the most magical part of the weekend was a procession along the avenue led by Boff and Casey – so many happy people.

After photographs, the non-stop music began; compeered by the incomparable *Lunge Dolphin* dressed in a shimmering blue jacket. First up teenage offspring band *The Zombie Squid Squad*. They were great. It was our turn next – we started with *Matchbox*. It was nothing special – nevertheless one of my favourite gigs ever. Next came a wonderful buffet, then in the evening the live karaoke band – what great fun. The disc jockeys took over and we danced into the small hours.

We swam in the meandering river every day. It was warm with a marvellous pool area and sandy shallows. On the Sunday morning we went for a swim up-river. There was me and several lithe American women and a couple of English ones, all of them experienced swimmers. I hadn't swum for years and I was a bit apprehensive. I managed to keep up though. We'd been swimming for more than ten minutes before I realised that I was the only boy in the office and I wondered if I'd crashed the party. An irate mother swan hissed at us as we swam by her and her babies. The water was deep and the current was strong and at times I was quietly anxious. What if I drown?

We swam for what seemed ages before reaching our destination, a low gravel bank island in the middle of the river. The women drifted ashore and one by one emerged goddess-like from the water – all svelte and glistening in the brilliant midday sun. They flicked their hair scattering iridescent droplets of water against the bright blue sky. It could have been a scene from a Bond movie.

I was last out and I felt like they were all watching me. I was hoping not to look like a complete dick. I wasn't out of breath or anything but when the moment came, my legs were like jelly and I couldn't actually stand up. After a brief quivering attempt, I dropped to my knees and I had to crawl out like some kind of lizard. The chance of looking cool was gone. They were all very polite and didn't laugh. At least my trunks didn't drop off. The swim back downstream was a blessed relief. The scenery along the river bank was magical. I went for a lie down when we got back.

I hadn't had the field that long and I'd treated myself to a *Tractor* magazine for my little holiday. There was a *Ladies on Tractors* page that made us all laugh. Pete has an old abandoned *David Brown* tractor and I took a photo of Lou and Alice sitting on it. I sent it in to Tractor hoping they would put it on their L.O.T. page but they didn't.

I made a video of the weekend. It opens with me, Khany and Boff heading towards the camera doing a silly run. I put a static camera on a tripod for the procession.

I left on the Monday morning and was sad to say goodbye to Khany and his lovely family. (AnnaMarie and his son Miles had arrived on a later flight.)

That wasn't the end though. Crusher and Emma came over to my house and we made a music video of a cover of Notsensibles' *The Telephone Rings Again*. Crusher picked up the bass line and had it down in a couple of takes. Emma sang backing vocals. Bish and I had recorded a drum and guitar backing track the night before. It was enormous good fun and the video turned out really well with daft dancing in the kitchen.

The long weekend finally ended a couple of days later when Louise and I went over to Leeds for a night out. The Americans were so gracious, insightful and well-rounded and it had been such an inspiring few days. A desire to go to America again was sparked and I resolved to make the effort and take Elias and Sam and visit Khany.

The customs process on arrival in the US is tedious: long queues; photos; fingerprints. The officials are officious. Khany met us in his white 66 Buick Riviera.

After a twenty-minute drive, we were back at his house. AnnaMarie, Sophia and Miles were there. It was bizarre. It was as if we'd stepped out of our front door in the morning and into Khany's living room in Florida. It was warm and muggy and starting to rain. They live in a wonderful stylish house on the shore of a lake.

We went swimming. The water was like a warm bath.
'Are there alligators in here?'
'Probably, but they won't bother you.'

It was OK being an untourist for a week. We went to a rehearsal of Khany's avant-garde band *Obliterati* at a studio in Orlando. (I filmed a couple of songs).

We had breakfast in an ordinary diner.

Sophia and I assembled an aluminium jetty ladder after a trip to *Skycraft* to look for stainless steel bolts.

Khany and I changed the front wheel on his custom vintage Harley.

We drove through the streets and swamps of Florida in his wonderful old Cadillacs. On one occasion we pushed his magnificent white *Elderado Brougham* across a red traffic light in the balmy night heat when it ran out of petrol on our way back from Sanford.

We drifted down a crystal clear spring-water river through tropical terrain on black rubber inner tubes and watched an orange and black striped snake swimming underneath AnnaMarie.

We watched the heads of strange prehistoric-looking mermaid-tailed creatures rising from a swampy estuary in the humid dusk.

We stood on a wooden jetty overlooking a backwater creek amidst swarms of mosquitoes and watched the shadowy outline of an alligator gliding by.

An episode one day summed up a fundamental difference between the UK and the USA. We were walking down the main street in Sanford when I happened to mention that neither me, Elias or Sam had ID with us. AnneMarie was visibly shocked. Clearly it's unthinkable for Americans not to carry ID with them whereas it's not something that bothers us much in the UK.

It was wonderful getting a glimpse of their ordinary everyday American life. The highlight of the fortnight was playing a little gig at *Uncle Lou's*, a little bar in Orlando. Me the lads and Khany got together a forty-minute set. We borrowed a lovely old Gretsch for Sam and I bought a second-hand *Squier* Strat in mint condition for $109. Elias played drums. Me, my friend and my boys playing a gig IN AMERICA.

After us was soul singer *Eugene Snowdon*. He asked me to get up and play in his band which was a wonderful thrill. The highlight was when we played *Wang Dang Doodle* which Sam and I sang and he joined in on the chorus. That's the bit I still struggle to believe – singing harmonies with a real black soul singer. What a thrill. On our last night in Florida we were hoping to make a music video for Khany's rockabilly band *The Wildtones*. It got cancelled at the last minute but we still did some filming at his house. There's a hilarious scene where he gets donked on the head by a frying pan (painstakingly made out of papier mache and realistically painted by AnnaMarie). There's also a daft dancing scene. Hopefully we'll use the footage one day. In order to transport the guitar on the plane, I'd unbolted the neck and was planning to put the two halves of the guitar in Elias's suitcase. We filmed a scene with Khany just playing the neck of the guitar. The camera is focused on the neck then pans down to the non-existent body – very funny.

For our second week, we'd booked an apartment way out in *Bayside* in Queens. We got a flight to JFK then a train from Penn Station. From there, unsure of the buses, we walked all the way up Corporal Kennedy Street to our destination. It was a lovely apartment – clean and modern with the helpful owner living downstairs. It was late by the time we got there and I set off to find a shop to buy food. There was a precinct close by. As I walked up the street in the semi-darkness, I saw someone approaching – a man in his forties. I was nervous. What if I get mugged? I needn't have worried. New York is the safest city I've ever been in and the public transport is second to none.

I had a gig at *Sidewalk Cafe* in the East Village on the Thursday night. I'd got it through a friend of my old muso mate John Donaldson. I was extremely apprehensive about it. I don't like playing on my own without a band. The gig was late at night to an audience of about twenty people. I was so incredibly nervous at first that I could hardly get through the first song. It was OK. I was glad it was over though. I could relax for the rest of the holiday. I'm not a tourist and I'm not mega keen on big cities. My holiday is to walk and walk and that's what I did. Up and down. Across and across. The Museum of Modern Art was amazing – all those famous paintings under one roof. *The Starry Night* was incredible, surrounded with a circle of viewers and its own dedicated guard.

Khany and Sophia drove up all the way from Orlando on the Friday night. There was a motorbike convention and Khany had his Harley in the back of the van. On the Saturday we drove up to Mohegan Lake to see his friends Paul and Natascha. They live in a lovely house overlooking the lake. Paul took us to see a mechanic friend of his who had lots of vintage American cars dotted around the woods outside his house. There were a couple of VWs and we talked air-cooled engines. On the Sunday we went to *The Met.* What an amazing place. There was a wonderful *Sargent* exhibition on. We got there late and had nowhere near enough time to see it all before it closed at five-thirty.

We'd driven down to New York in Khany's van and parked in the outskirts. After going to The Met, we went for a meal then parted company on a crowded subway train. It was like a film scene. I was sad. I might never see them again. I wanted to walk on the *High Line* but the lads wouldn't come with me. They just wanted to go back to the flat.

'Which stop do we get off for Penn Station?'

I thought to myself, 'I've brought you all the way to New York and all you want to do is go back to the fucking flat. You won't even spend a couple of hours with me – fuck off.'

'The next one,' I lied.

I walked and walked and walked. I can understand why a lot of people like New York. Cities are all the same to me though – crowded expensive lonely places. New York isn't that hot on public toilets either. There was some rubbish neatly piled at the intersection of a street and an avenue and a women was putting a chair on it and accidentally caught me with the leg. 'Oh sorry,' she said. I was too slow/shy/dull/stupid to strike up a conversation. I carried on walking until I was exhausted then got the train to Bayside and walked up Bell Boulevard back to the flat.

Originally we'd planned to go to America in February but my dad got ill. He'd died in March. We finally went in September. It was a strange trip. Two post-teenage lads and their dad. It wasn't sweet and pretty. It was rather spiky at times. I think there was some subliminal grieving going on during those long walks along streets and avenues. Khany had talked a lot about his parents too.

Three days later we were home. I didn't sleep a wink on the flight back. I watched the progress of the plane on the

TV screen on the back of the seat in front. Sam put on the black eye mask provided by the airline and slept in typical dormouse fashion. Elias and I did maths problems for his forthcoming engineering course.

The ranch was all wild and secret and beautiful when we got back – overgrown and somehow silently confident in its ability to thrive regardless of my input.

15. Cardiff (and beyond).

Friday 14th August. Table, top of ranch.

I get off the train at Cardiff and Thomo is getting off too. He's wearing a parka and a Fred Perry tee-shirt. I saw him as soon as I got on at Manchester. He had his Sunday paper sprawled over a table. I looked in his direction but he didn't see me and I didn't want to bother him. My seat was a few rows behind. He walked past a couple of times during the journey and I looked in his direction but he still didn't see me (or maybe he was ignoring me?)

I love train journeys. All I do is look out of the window and have my packed lunch like a child on a school trip. I adore just looking at the fleeting images flashing by. It's one of the only times that I can just sit and watch and do nothing. I say hello as soon as we get off.

He tuts. 'Were you sitting a few seats behind me?'
'Er, yes.' I'm too reserved my own good. He hails from Cardiff and he's off to see his mum and dad.

We're both A&E consultants and we're going to the annual conference of *The Royal College of Emergency Medicine* which starts tomorrow. We did some of our training together. I'm an imposter because I work for myself through an agency and it suits me just fine. I've started doing most of my shifts at the hospital where Thomo works.

After leaving the old place, the first thing I did was have a wonderful break, working at the things that mattered: the ranch; music; building guitar amps; writing and so on. Various twats made snide remarks because of their expectation that I should be earning shit loads of money in 'a proper job'. None of them understand. They're all caught up in their bourgeois delusions and presumed I was being a dosser so they can bugger off. I've abandoned the patriarchal Victorian work/servitude/usury model of work – it's shite. I prefer Don Juan's approach. 'Your time for my time.'

I made sure we had a lavish Christmas and I bought lots of presents for everybody. Everyone had a big stocking. I bought Elias and Sam a Hofner bass and a Danelectro guitar respectively. I'd hidden them and left an envelope on the mantelpiece with a cryptic riddle in it. They had to solve the riddle to find the guitars. I think a bit of mystery and imagination is important in life. My dad had always given us that with his storytelling. He'd read *The Hobbit* to

Michael and me when we were little. We later both devoured *Lord of The Rings*. In due course, I read the Hobbit to my kids. It was probably a bit early because Sam was only six or so. When I'd finished it, I told them about Lord of The Rings.

'Read it to us, read it to us.'
'You're a bit too young and it's very long and complicated. There are three volumes – it's better to wait a couple of years.'

I relented and I did read it to them; all three volumes. It just so happened that the first film came out as we'd finished reading the first book *The Fellowship of the Ring*. When we got back from seeing it, I fired two arrows at once through their bedroom door just like Legolas in the film. (We'd only recently moved into the house and we were planning to replace the cheap modern doors with original ones). I believe in children being allowed to be children. I made them wooden swords and shields and bows and arrows and they had Swiss army knives. There's too much nimby-pimby political correctness in this day and age.

We've always had a family fascination with archery. It began when my dad made us a bow out of an old butter barrel – we must only have been five or six. He and his brother had bows and arrows in their youth. He used to tell us the story of the battle of Agincourt. I remember having *Enid Blyton's* Tales of Robin Hood. The post office up the road sold books and my mum used to take us up on Saturday mornings to choose one. The famous story of Robin Hood splitting an arrow at an archery contest actually comes from The Buddha's life. Before he gave up everything to seek enlightenment, he was an affluent prince and an accomplished archer.

I have the script for a novel in my head. It's called *Gunman, Bowman,* and is about a young lad fascinated with archery who takes on a nutter about to embark on a massacre with a *Kalashnikov.* Michael and I still have bows. There's a valley up on the moors above town with a stream and a gnarled ash tree. We used to go up there. We could shoot across the small valley at the opposite bank and not lose our arrows. I remember using an orange as a target and finally hitting it after shooting at it hundreds of times. Archery as a metaphor for focus is universally used in lots of spiritual traditions and it's definitely big in Buddhism. Eugene Herrigel's *Zen in The Art of Archery* is wonderful.

Later on, Elias, Sam, Matt and Tyler would have mammoth Lord of the Rings sessions spending all night watching the entire box set.

My dad frequently spoke about my grandad's time in the First World War and he had a story about a real-life ring. It was a snake ring with a diamond for the eye. My grandad was in the East Lancs Regiment and was wounded at Gallipoli. He'd been given the ring when he went off to war and my dad reckoned that it was a talisman that protected him. Given the numbers of casualties in the East Lancs regiment maybe there was some truth in it.

My dad often mentioned the ring and I had a vague memory of having seen it once. For some reason, I thought it was silver. Not long before he died, he asked about it. He reckoned that he'd given it to me but I had no memory of it. We presumed that it was lost. He'd always said that it was a special ring and that it was to be passed down to the oldest son. After a lot of searching, Kit (my brother's wife) found it in a jug and it came to me. It's actually gold and very beautiful. There are two snakes intertwined and two diamonds for their eyes. One has been replaced by a much cruder modern one.

I have a bit of a story in my head where the ring is magic and we are a family with a similar destiny to all those characters who helped get Frodo through Mordor. We're all various warriors and heroes. Obviously I'm king and Louise is queen. Rachel is an elven princess. Crown prince Elias is Aragorn-like and Sam; Matt; Tyler; Garth; Bryn; Glasgow; Jack; Deano; Pete; Ryde; Noonan; Danny Hobbs; Zord and Enty are all great warrior princes in our fight against evil. Bish; Michael; Ruth; the Welsh wizard

Taff and his wife Ann; Fran and Jude; Tricia and Dewy; Fenny and Jenny sit with me on the guiding council. My Aunt Christine (also auntie to Deano) is our wise and witty matriarch. We'll take on the orcs, trolls and goblins anytime.

When my dad died we scattered his ashes over the old farm on the moors above the town. It's all overgrown now and quite difficult to spot. The path used to go right past it but the council made a load of new footpaths and now you have to climb over a fence to get to it. It was Michael's idea to recite Tennyson's *Ulysses*. My dad always appreciated poetry and drama and he loved the sea. He was into sailing all his life.

> *... Death closes all, but somewhere ere the end,*
> *Some work of noble note may yet be done...*
>
> *The long day wanes: The slow moon climbs:*
> *The deep moans round with many voices.*
> *Come my friends, tis not too late to seek a newer world.*
> *Push off, and sitting well in order*
> *Smite the sounding furrows;*
> *For my purpose holds to sail beyond the sunset,*
> *And the baths of all the western stars, until I die.*

I see more of Christine since my dad died. She's always been a breath of fresh air. She was a primary school teacher before she retired. She taught Boff and Bish. She and my uncle Ivor were very close to my mum. I once bumped into them at the general hospital when I was working there as a house officer. Christine later told me that Ivor had been moved to tears when he saw me, saying, 'His mum would have been so proud.'

Christine was always a live wire at family gatherings (and still is). With her razor wit she was more than a match for my dad when he came out with his outrageous bombastic attention-seeking statements. She has a vast knowledge and appreciation of English literature; along with my cousin Judith she's one of my muses. She's given me endless encouragement in writing my book.

She did her teacher training at a college in Liverpool. Towards the end, she was sent to a very rough school in Bootle. The class was anarchic and one big girl in particular was constantly disruptive. Finally on one cataclysmic Friday afternoon Christine decided that despite her best efforts, teaching wasn't for her. She was trying to talk to the class about *The Wife of Usher's Well*, a ballad that had been passed down orally for several generations before ever being written down. It tells the story of a mother who sends her three strong sons to sea. The mother later learns that they have all been killed.

... 'I wish the wind may never cease,
Nor fashes in the flood,
Til my three sons come hame to me,
In earthly flesh and blood.

After Christine had read out the poem, as anticipated, the big-mouthed disrupter stood up. Christine expected the worst. There was a pause before the girl said, 'Read it again Miss.' That was the turning point.

... 'Fare ye weel, my mother dear!
Fareweel to barn and byre!
And fare ye weel, the bonny lass
That kindles my mother's fire.

After she'd read the poem a second time she asked the class: 'What kind of poem is it?' Just one shy little boy put his hand up. 'It's a love story Miss.'

After a wonderful break from medicine I joined an agency. I had no intention of giving up just yet. I had the lofty idea of working all over the country in the busiest A&E departments – Glasgow, London, Nottingham. That idea didn't last long. The first shift that came up was at a fairly local hospital in North Manchester. It was convenient so I ended up working there and doing enough shifts to get by. It was just an ordinary district general hospital with decent ordinary folk doing their best. The consultants there (Jimmy, Jim and Mark) and I had several productive conversations about tractors, farms and vehicles in general. I remember making a comment about doctors who know how to take out engines. I was loving working for myself. I had complete freedom and flexibility and was making enough to get by.

One day a shift came up at the hospital where Thomo works. I'd been a medical student and a senior house officer there. I knew most of the consultants. A few of us had trained together. The building had changed beyond recognition after various upgrades but a lot of the nurses were still there and they all remembered me. They'd seen Notsensibles when we were on telly and they'd seen my daft John Lee Hartley videos.

There were a few little coincidences and omens going on which I tried to ignore. There are a few musos and guitarists there. One of the nurse practitioners has a Hofner Verithin. There are three other people with old VW vans. One day, we were talking about rockabilly and Angelina looked up in her usual deadpan inscrutable way and said, 'I've got a double bass.' I'd fitted in well when I was first there and there was still something of that old feeling about the place. Best of all though, Thomo had heard of The Frantic Elevators. NO-ONE has heard of the Frantic Elevators. There's an air of quiet common sense and none of the nonsense that existed at the old place. The managers are very supportive and the relationship between

A&E and the acute physicians, the anaesthetists and the intensivists is fantastic. People are singing from the same hymn sheet most of the time.

Double bass ownership and Frantic Elevators recognition are very impressive credentials indeed and significant omens that are difficult to ignore. Ollie works there. I was thrilled recently when his wife's band *The Hayes Sisters* was on Woman's Hour.

Even when you're a locum doctor, you still have to complete the same amount of brownie point box-ticking. It's called 'CPD'. I can think of a nice vernacular alternative but it actually stands for *Continuing Professional Development*. Going to a conference gives you a big chunk of CPD points.

When I was working at the old place, going to a conference was a non-starter. I didn't have the time or inclination. Now I was self-employed, it was a nice little working holiday and I could claim all my expenses back. I was particularly interested in seeing Cardiff because my dad had been stationed at St Athan near there when he was in the Air Force. He talked with great fondness about Tiger Bay and the docks. He used to authoritatively say that Cardiff docks were where curry was first introduced to the UK. I've no idea whether it's true or not. He had a bit of a flair for exaggeration.

The conference was in the Mercure Hotel and I was staying there. I met up with Thomo on the Monday morning. Angelina, Stibbs and Caroletta were there too. Very flatteringly they'd been trying to persuade me to take a job but I'd learned my lesson the hard way. I just wasn't cut out for the rat race. Locuming suited me just fine. I pointed out that I just couldn't go back to doing night shifts and on-calls. 'That's fine,' they said. All the shifts I was doing were 12-8s and they suited me perfectly because I could fit them round the rest of my daily routine. 'Just do 12-8 shifts then,' they said.

The conference was enjoyable. There was a jazz band playing in the bar on the Sunday night. I expected it to be filled with rumbustious A&E consultants behaving outrageously but it was empty. How very disappointing. On the Monday evening, Angelina, Stibbs, Thomo and I went for a meal in a nice Italian on the edge of Tiger bay. I imagined how different it would have been when my dad was there. Thomo and I joked about the ubiquitous bronze statues of Cardiff.

The next day we walked into town during the lunch break. Thomo was going to get some presents for his kids and I was headed for Spillers record shop, reputed to be the oldest in the world. I bought a Bill Callaghan record. I'd never heard of him until he'd done a wonderful Marc Riley session a couple of weeks previously. He did an exquisite song called *Small Plane*. The live version was better than the album version. Thomo is a bit of a muso on the quiet. He saw The Smiths play in Newport. He told me that Bill Callaghan previously played in a band called Smog.

On the last night, we were in the hotel bar. There was background music and it was The Frantic Elevators singer's band. Thomo said 'Your bezzie's on'. Next a different version of The Pogues *Dirty Old Town* came on. It was quieter with a girl singing alternate verses and backing vocals. There was a dreamy clarinet solo. I don't like The Pogues. I don't like folk-rock of any description but I quite liked this. Thomo pointed out that it was the original version by Ewan McColl. I'd always presumed that the *Dirty Old Town* was somewhere in Ireland but apparently not.

> *I found my love where the gaslight falls.*
> *Dreamed a dream by the old canal.*

It sounds like my home town. Our old house was by the canal. We had another conversation about me taking 'a proper job'. 'I'm saving all my lovin' for someone who's lovin' me,' I jokingly said. Thomo comically raised his eyebrows. 'Not in that way,' I hastily added.

Back home, I put the finishing touches to my third guitar amplifier. When the terrifying moment came to switch it on for the first time, it blew a capacitor in the fixed bias circuit – I'd tried to be clever and make it switchable between fixed and cathode bias – only amp nerds will know what I'm talking about. The amp is my most ambitious so far – a thirty-watter. Like the other two, it's based on a late 50s Fender design, but I've added a few tweaks of my own. I couldn't work out why it had blown the capacitor and the bloke who I used to take amps to had retired, so it sat on top of the type cabinet for a year.

One day, I was watching amp nerd vids on the internet when I chanced across *In a Vacuum* – a wonderful little film about valve amp repairer Roland Lumby. He was very droll and witty and referred to all guitarists as *Loons* which made me laugh. He mentioned fixing *Elbow's* amps. I tracked him down and in another serendipitous twist, he lives ten minutes walk away from work – yet another little omen that keeps dragging me back to that dirty old town. He's far more droll and witty in real life than he is on the video. We talked about our times on the Manchester music scene. He used to do the sound for bands and did the PA at *The Electric Circus*. There's a great ten-inch album – *Short Circuit – Live at The Electric Circus*. I bought it on blue vinyl when it first came out (part of the punk scene was a fashion for coloured vinyl). It has two great Fall tracks on it and an early Joy Division track.

'Who's Hartley?' He said when he saw the badge on the amp.

'I am,' I said.

'Did you build that?'

'Yes.'

'Good lad.'

'What are those piddling little things?' he said, when he saw the power capacitors. 'It's the twenty-first century – the reason they used little capacitors in 1959 was that they couldn't make big ones.'

'Oh.'

'How old are you?'

'Phew, you're too old to rival me.'

He fixed the amp and it sounds exquisite – as pure as pure can be. It has a 1959 Jensen P15 speaker that I bought from America.

He also fixed the beautiful 1960s *Voix de Son Maitre* record player that Louise bought me for Christmas a few years ago. At first he said, 'throw it in the bin', but he relented. It gave him an electric shock. Ha. He'd mentioned that he liked dub so I took a Lee Perry 7" round and his wife Jules made a little YouTube vid of us chilling to it. I took the record player into work and played Jimmy Hughes' *Neighbour Neighbour* for Thomo – it's one of my fave R&B 7s.

Cary and Caroletta came into the office and were clearly impressed. It's a shame that the social side has disappeared from hospital life. I'm sure we could knock up a decent little Rock & Roll band between us.

Back when I was a house officer, Vincent did a gig at the hospital where I was working. It was on a Saturday night in the diabetes day unit building. That kind of thing wouldn't be allowed now. In those days medicine had an integral social life. There were thriving doctors' messes and wild parties, but not any more.

The NHS talks a lot about recruitment and retention; sometimes I don't think they're very good at it. There are desperate shortages of doctors and nurses; the reasons are complicated. I have to say that there are some places that couldn't recruit and retain a turd out of a toilet. It's not rocket science. It's an art of skilful communication and perceptive intuition. It's about making people feel good about themselves – about having things in the workplace not necessarily related to work that can ease the flow, music being the perfect example. And good food! – the way to a woman's heart is through her stomach. It's about talking to people and asking them how they're getting on and giving them somewhere of their own to hang their coat. It depends on face-to-face contact and it costs very little. All the major successful companies have nailed it, but the NHS doesn't seem to have fully grasped the concept.

The antitheses of recruitment and retention are FIOFs (Fucking Irritating Online Forms) and AIEs (Automated Impersonal Emails) which are sent to your home e-mail address telling you that you haven't done your hand-washing test this year, so you can't have any study leave. These impersonal techniques are a guaranteed way to get rid of employees. Fair enough, the reality is that people in the NHS are just so overwhelmingly busy, under-staffed and under-funded that often there's no time for this recruitment and retention stuff. Still, there's always room for improvement.

Despite all its difficulties, the NHS remains one of the finest fairest employers and provides a wonderful service. It's heartbreaking to see it destroyed and privatised by a bunch of millionaire twats who can all afford private healthcare.

Around 25% of our tax contribution to the NHS goes purely on interest and profits to bankers and global conglomerates via private finance initiatives (PFIs). PFIs are a travesty. They are a method of providing funds for major capital investments where private firms are contracted to complete and manage public projects such as hospitals and schools. In return, they charge obscene amounts of interest over decades (16% of the annual budget at one of Manchester's largest healthcare trusts). They are crippling the NHS. I sometimes ask myself at what point did we all become so fucking dull and spineless. So bourgeois and blasé? At what point do people get up and do something about saving the caring fabric of society?

My revolution would be very carefully thought out and no-one would be harmed. All the monstrous bankers and billionaire crooks would be completely stripped of their assets and given turquoise tracksuits, white socks and grey slip-on shoes. Their wealth would be redistributed to build a fair and equitable society and they would be parachuted into the areas of greatest need. The team that are destroying our NHS would be flown into Syria and Yemen and other areas of desperation where their expertise would be put to good use. Their giant guzzling four-wheel drives would be confiscated and they would have the choice of a unicycle or a tricycle.

I was more than happy doing locum shifts, but part of me was beginning to feel guilty about not being a part of the NHS and despite my better judgement, I started to think about taking a proper job. The real crux was finding such a great bunch of truly inspiring people to work with. Maybe there's a corner of the NHS that accepts renegades like me after all? I imaged having a desk next to Thomo's and we'd have a little record player and a few singles.

My daughter Rachel had a show for the final year of her degree. It turned out it was in The Dirty Old Town in the masonic hall. As we approached in the car, we were waiting at some traffic lights. I happened to glance left and there was a stone plaque saying:

This hospital was enlarged in the year 1886...

Another darned omen.

The potatoes are all in storage in the stable and the onions are drying out. The figs are beginning to ripen and there's a bumper crop on the tree. I still can't believe that they grow up here – there are more every year. I'm taking home a carrier bag of food every other day – runner beans, courgettes, plums, apples, broccoli, kale, dill, basil, parsley. Am I the farmer?

16. The Presentation

Sat 5th September. Type cabinet, back room.

As I anticipated, the long weary job application process involved lots of FIOFs and AIEs and to add spice, it was administered by a private firm. I gritted my teeth and got on with it. I was invited to an interview. One of the FIOFs was psychometric testing with lots of twatty questions that seemed to have no relevance to me. 'Are you a sporty team player or a solitary dark horse?' – 'er... neither.' It was all going to plan but I was still feeling very doubtful. Then I got an email:

As part of your interview for the above position you will be asked to undertake a 10 minute presentation entitled "The role of the Consultant Emergency Physician in ensuring the delivery of safe, high quality care in challenging times." Can you please email a copy of your presentation to...

I'd-rather-shit-in-my-hands-and-clap alarm bells rang. This was one condescending patronising step too far. Surely at this level an interview is a two-way process? There's a limit to the amount of pointless faceless bureaucracy I can cope with. I had butterflies in my stomach but also a great sense of relief. What was I thinking? Had I not learned my lesson? Phew – what a relief.

I did nothing for a couple of days and spent a wonderful weekend on the ranch, pottering and tidying. The routine of going up there regularly and repeating the same chores and observing nature is very comforting and grounding. It's a great environment for contemplation and thinking through problems. Lots of plants were still doing well and I was still harvesting lots of stuff.

I just couldn't resist. I couldn't stop myself. I'm a sucker for cryptic detail and the thing that clinched it was that they called me Dear Candidate with a capital 'C'. It made me sound like a rapper. I also completely disagreed with being asked to provide a copy of the presentation before giving it.

I replied:

Dear... Thank you for calling me Candidate. You make me sound like a rapper...

I said that if I was going to do a presentation, I'd do it on a topic of my choice in a style of my choice – namely as a video. No way was I going to give them a copy beforehand. I pointed out that at consultant level, an interview was a two-way process and that their faceless bureaucratic approach may well put a lot of people off. I then included a link to the YouTube video of my song *Good Job, Proper Job*. I wrote the song years ago after a chance encounter with an old friend. We were talking about the work-life balance conundrum. He'd given up being a chartered surveyor to work in a herbalist's shop. He told me about George Orwell's *Keep the Aspidistra Flying*. I've got a copy, but I've never read it – VBL bass player Karl Eden gave it me. The theme that comes across is giving up being a slave to the money-god rat race in order to do what you love, even if it turns you into a pauper – right up my street. Bish and I went to town on the video – it's definitely one of our daftest and most surreal.

Too many memos getting on my tits
Too many jumped-up paper shovelling shits
Too many computers telling me what to do
Too many guidelines and protocols

Good Job, Proper Job.

Too many managers and jumped-up clerks
Too much commuting on motorways
Too many frustrating fucked-up days
Too much bureaucracy getting in the way
Good Job, Proper Job.

Musicians seem to have a compulsion to declare their videos as 'Official.' Rock & Roll surely is the antithesis of official? Our videos are definitely unofficial.

A few days later at work, Boyce took me to one side. He's tall and quietly spoken with rugged Colin Firth good looks. We worked together back in the day. We were both registrars and we were both doing research with Iona who is now deservedly a professor.

'You've really pissed them off. OK it's funny, but unless you do some serious arse-kissing, I think you can forget it.'

The person who was pissed off was a director overseeing the interview process. She doesn't work in the emergency department.

'Should I withdraw?' I said.
'It's up to you.'
'I suppose I've pissed on my chips.'

I left it at that. I didn't do any arse-kissing, but I emailed the director explaining my point of view. It would have been the easiest thing in the world just to withdraw but I couldn't. My terrier instinct doesn't let go and once I embark on something, I see it through. The interview was on the following Monday. I decided to wait until close of play on Friday. If I hadn't heard anything from them by then, I'd go ahead and do the presentation.

They actually sent me an email on the Thursday asking me if I would be attending for the interview. I replied, saying that I would.

That was it then. There's a fine line between having the courage to speak out and stand up for what you believe in and arrogance. When you have no self-confidence, it takes many years to develop self-belief. I was in the excruciatingly uncomfortable position of having to do a ten-minute video before Monday morning. Video making is a very time-consuming process.

The starting point was the backing track. Bish and I both love Jimmy McGriff's *Bump de Bump*. It's a sixties shuffling swinging instrumental with Jimmy McGriff playing organ – it was a staple of the mod & Twisted Wheel era. It has a fantastic drum beat and Bish has spent ages learning it. I thought that we'd do a live recording of it with me playing bass. Coincidentally and serendipitously however, a record arrived in the post that day. It was *Going down for the last time* by Ronnie Keaton and the Ocean Liners. It's wonderful seventies funk with impeccable drumming. I'd been trying to get a copy for years but it's very rare and expensive. One day, I spotted a 'reissue' and bought it. We used that for the backing track instead. I quickly learned the bass line and we recorded it live with a static camera filming us. Bish put on an afro wig and a piece of white card in his mouth to emulate perfect teeth. He stared at the camera for the whole ten minutes playing a crisp funk beat. I later over-dubbed a funky choppy guitar and a keyboard.

The opening scene shows an alarm clock on my bedside table set at ten o'clock. It goes off and the camera pans to me sitting bolt upright in bed, having overslept. I'm wearing a daft wig and a false moustache and beard. Elias filmed it. The next scene is a close-up of Bish drumming then a current newspaper headline spinning in like in old films. It says:

CASH BID TO HALT STRIKE – 371 consultants sign letter warning of A&E staff crisis.

It just so happened to be the time of the junior doctors' strike. A couple of weeks earlier the annual scientific conference of The Royal College of Emergency Medicine took place at Manchester Central immediately before the Tory Party conference. It was swarming with police getting ready for the Tories and the junior doctors were demonstrating outside The Midland Hotel.

During one of the lectures the college president came in and pointed out that the college delegates and speakers would be going into The Midland Hotel for their annual black-tie dinner when the junior doctors were demonstrating outside. He advised prudence if approached by the press. He had been mentioned by Jeremy Corbyn at Prime Minister's question time that week. Personally, I thought it was a wasted golden opportunity to raise some publicity for the plight of Emergency Medicine and show our support for the juniors. If I'd been in charge (never even a microscopic possibility), I would have organised a slick military-style operation to show the vile *unt health secretary and his cronies that no-one fucks with the nation's Emergency Medicine Consultants. Here's how it would have panned out:

After the main meal, the massed dinner-goers would have separated into two groups – one by the hotel side entrance and one by the front entrance. The junior doctors outside would have been tipped off. At this point, there would be just a few coppers keeping an eye on them. At precisely the same moment, both groups would swarm forth from the hotel, shouting and screaming loudly in a Viking style. They would surround the demonstration in an instant and push over the astonished coppers. They would then unite in a rousing NHS-saving battle cry that could be heard across half of Manchester.

The dazed plods would immediately get on their radios and there would be the inevitable disproportionate response, with droves of paramilitarised rozzers swarming in, in disorganised panic. The ubiquitous 'copter would soon appear. We would have several carefully placed cameras filming it all.

The next morning, we would inevitably be front page news for all the right reasons. Of course it would never happen but it's fun to imagine it. We're all far too well behaved and obedient.

After the conference, I got the bus home. As it moved slowly past the Midland hotel, I watched the demonstrators intently. They looked so young – all decent hard-working people trying to do the best for their patients. I took a photo of one of them holding a placard saying, *'Fuck off Dave.'*

One of the consequences of the junior doctors' strike was that the consultants had to provide cover. I didn't hear a single one of my colleagues complain. For many specialities this was a real challenge as many consultants haven't done the jobs that junior doctors do for many years.

For us, it was very pleasant indeed. In emergency medicine, the consultants are the last port of call for the most difficult tasks such as gaining venous access. It's a double-edged sword as we end up dealing with the most difficult challenging cases. Not only that, but we are constantly interrupted to deal with other issues including supporting the junior doctors and reviewing their patients. Paradoxically, their absence reduced our short-term work load and we had a very civilised day indeed, quietly seeing patients without interruption. The icing on the cake was the banter between us and the acute physicians. It was the highest quality politically incorrect intellectual banter anywhere ever. Heaven help any NHS-destroying politician caught in our cross-fire.

Back to The Presentation. The background throughout the video is faded footage of me and Bish playing the backing track interspersed with relevant photos (including *Fuck off Dave*). The guitar gets wilder towards the end. I couldn't resist one completely daft scene where I'm in the kitchen dressed in white bell bottoms, wearing an Afghan and a Bee Gees wig, standing on one leg and tunelessly playing a tin whistle. It's my little salute to pointless bureaucracy. Throughout the video, red bold text scrolls over the background. Right at the end, I address the points that they initially asked for, but before that I observe that we can't possibly deliver safe efficient care unless we address the catastrophic shortage of senior A&E doctors.

I point out what the PFIs and the moneyed elite are actually doing to the NHS and I talk about the valiant efforts of The College to try and tackle the problems. I mention the value of a social life in medicine and I mention all the above coincidences at the Scientific Conference. The whole thing takes me many non-stop hours and I'm exhausted by the end of it. Throughout the long arduous process, I keep thinking what I'm going to say to the director and I can't think of anything.

My interview is at ten o'clock, which is the worst possible time for commuting. I'm up at six and sitting in the car park by a quarter to eight for an excruciatingly uncomfortable two-hour wait. I don't do traffic jams or queuing up to pay inflated car park charges. I'm wearing my trusty dog tooth check suit with the obligatory Scotty dog cufflinks. It's pissing down with non-stop heavy rain.

The interview is in the seminar room right in the middle of the department. I'm there at precisely ten o'clock. Did I mention that I was pathologically punctual? There's a girl sitting outside looking very nervous and I say to her, 'Are you here for the interview?' I already knew that they were interviewing someone else. 'Yes,' she replies. 'What time's your interview?' I ask. 'Ten o'clock,' she says. 'That's funny, so is mine.' I knock on the door and Thomo answers it. He, Angelina and Caroletta are interviewing along with a girl from Human Resources and the Director who hasn't arrived yet. It's a priceless moment. Clearly they weren't expecting me and they all look utterly dumbfounded.

Obviously there's been a monumental Human Resources fuck-up. It makes me feel much better. I tell them that they sent me an email last week asking whether I would be attending for the interview and that I'd confirmed that I would. Thomo asks me to wait outside. 'No way am I standing outside the headmaster's office like a naughty schoolboy,' I think to myself. I tell him that I'll wait outside the front entrance of the department.

I decide that I'll stay until 10.30 then fuck off. A few minutes later Katrina (our wonderful secretary) comes out and tells me they'll interview me at 11.30. Back to the car park. Once again, I walk in from the rain precisely on time. Thomo has already come to the front entrance to see if I'm there.

The director is late. When she arrives, I stare at her without blinking until she looks away. As I anticipated, she asks me about my email. She says I'm flippant and non-collegiate whatever that's supposed to mean. I respectfully point out that I'm a member of two Royal Colleges and that I've been to three conferences in the last eighteen months. She asks me if I have a presentation. I tell her that I have, but it might not be what she expects. I hand the memory stick to Thomo and I'm enormously relieved when it works (I have back-up copies). I watch the interviewers' faces intently as it plays and the sense of relief when it finishes is immense. I've done it. I've finished what I started. The rest is irrelevant. The director asks me if I have anything to say about my presentation.

'No.'

I have a few CD versions in my pocket to dramatically skim across the table when they ask for a copy, but they never do.

I've been to lots of medical interviews and I've been an interviewer a few times. It's a standard format with pre-decided questions. It's usually pretty straightforward.

'Do you have any questions?'

I reply, 'How much time do you spend in The Emergency Department?'

She asks me if I'd like to wait for their decision. Would I fuck. I can't get out fast enough – I'm out of there like a blue-arsed fly. 'Er, no thank you – I have other commitments.'

Two hours later I'm on the ranch – wiped out and relieved. It's still lashing with rain and it's all grey, wild, wet and magnificent. Up here, there are no quasi-military officials in ubiquitous hi-viz jackets. There are no cunts with clipboards. I don't have to endlessly struggle with a fucking irritating computer before I shovel the horse shit from the midden.

Angelina phones and offers me the job but points out that the director has insisted that it's a 12-month fixed-term contract. Fine. I can stomach a year.

17. Emergency 3

Table top of ranch. Sunday 20th September

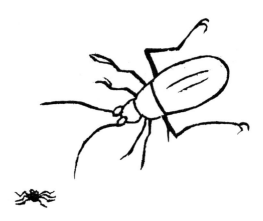

Ouch. I've foolishly tripped when skipping about carrying a bucket of water by the edge of the well and almost fallen in. I've scraped all my leg and bashed my side. It feels like I've broken a rib.

I once dislocated one of my toes coming down the stairs. I had the choice of going to A&E (oh no, I've been there all day) or popping it back myself. Crikey that was painful. My arms and face are frequently covered in scratches from the hawthorn and dog rose in the hedge. It's OK – my colleagues know about the ranch. I take excess produce to work and leave it in the staff room.

It's worth describing what happens in this country when someone is badly injured. In general, the term 'trauma' refers to stressful events. In medicine, it means injury.

As with any other branch of medicine, a lot of research has gone into trauma and there's a network in the north-west which Professor Yates set up. Some of my colleagues are involved in the work there and Iona is research director. Her professorship is in trauma. She was my mentor when I first started working in A&E years ago. When I came back to A&E after briefly trying general practice (I hated it), she was at my registrar interview. She'd given me and my friend a few suggestions beforehand. During the interview, she fixed me with her gentle smile and her eyes were shining with kindness. My friend and I both got jobs.

Research tells us that the best results in trauma come about when it's dealt with at a centre of concentrated expertise – nothing surprising about that. A few years ago trauma management was reviewed and rationalised. Now, every region has a major trauma centre (MTC) along with a number of trauma units.

Research also tells us that outcomes are better in trauma when led by a senior doctor who is designated 'Trauma Team Leader' (TTL). TTLs have to be trauma trained and be Fellows of The Royal College of Emergency Medicine (or College of Orthopaedics). MTCs are required to have a

TTL on the premises twenty-four hours a day (or available within thirty minutes). In today's climate of senior doctor shortages, this is a major challenge.

The ambulance service plays a crucial part in the initial management of trauma patients. They deliver the initial emergency care which includes immobilising the patient on a spinal board (or 'scoop') and keeping their neck still using collar and blocks in order to avoid any further damage. They will also gain IV access and give morphine.

The crew have to decide whether an incident constitutes a major trauma and they have a list of criteria to guide them in this. Once this decision is made, they make a call to ambulance control who in turn call our standby phone in the resuscitation room. We are given a standard amount of information, which includes mechanism of injury, the patient's vital signs and estimated time of arrival.

On the basis of the information from the standby call, the TTL decides who else to call to help manage the injured patient. The commonest scenario is an isolated head injury. We will then put out a 'head call' which goes to an anaesthetist and an ODP (operating department practitioner). If a patient is seriously injured, we will put out a full trauma call which in addition will go out to orthopaedic surgeons, general surgeons and the CT department.

Whilst waiting for the patient to arrive, we prepare all our drugs and equipment in a dedicated resuscitation bay. The TTL designates members of the team to deal with specific aspects of care: 'airway, breathing and circulation'.

When the patient arrives, we get them over onto the hospital trolley and get a full handover from the ambulance crew. If the patient is conscious, I always lean over them so that they can see my face. I try and reassure them that they are in the best place and I tell them that there will be several people fussing over them for quite some time. Often, in the hubbub, people forget to explain to the patient what is happening. It must be very frightening for them when they're strapped to a board and they can't move their head – particularly if they're in pain.

The first few minutes are crucial and involve a rapid decision-making process which boils down to:

1. Do we need to do a full trauma CT?
2. Do we need to anaesthetise the patient before going to CT?
3. Is the patient stable enough to go to CT or do they need to go straight to theatre?
4. Is the patient bleeding significantly and do we need to activate the major haemorrhage protocol?

These decisions are part of the primary survey which attempts to quickly identify any severe and life-threatening injuries.

The guidelines for doing a full body CT are very clear but ultimately the decision is down to the TTL. The bottom line is that a mechanism of injury which has caused a significant injury in one area of the body may well have caused hidden injuries elsewhere so our threshold is low.

Once we've done the initial stabilisation, which includes taking blood samples and giving painkillers and fluids, we go to CT as quickly as possible.

Even if the patient doesn't require an emergency anaesthetic (known as a 'Rapid Sequence Induction or RSI), the anaesthetist and ODP often come with us and they're an extremely useful part of the team, freeing up some of our emergency department resources. In the CT department, we study the screen as the initial images flash by. Sometimes we can see major injuries such as bleeding in the brain. We can phone the neurosurgeons or other relevant speciality direct from CT to speed things up. All the CTs are rapidly reported by a trauma radiologist.

Sometimes the patient will go direct to theatre from CT. If they're stable enough, we'll go back to the department. We carry on the management by doing a more detailed assessment (known as a secondary survey) and we'll make phone calls to other relevant specialities.

When we're dealing with a severely injured patient, not only does it involve the trauma team but also several other doctors, nurses and emergency practitioners. Invariably a trauma call occupies the TTL for at least a couple of hours and the rest of the department can get very busy as a large chunk of our resources are directed to managing the trauma.

The whole process is a triumph of teamwork and organisation based on the best science and technology. Patients have the greatest possible chance of surviving their injuries. Due to the progress in automotive safety and trauma research, people are surviving accidents that even a few years ago would have killed them. It's one of the many magnificent achievements of the NHS.

It's impossible to describe the pressures of working in an emergency department. We have to be trained to deal with emergencies but there's so much more going on. A lot of it is social medicine and there's all the bureaucracy – fighting with other specialities trying to get them to accept patients and so on. Patients on ambulance trolleys queuing down the corridor waiting to offload. No beds in the hospital for patients to go to after they've been seen by us. Patients with long-term complicated conditions who come to us because they're not satisfied with their GP or the treatment that they've had elsewhere.

Somewhere, somehow the stresses and strains must take their toll and we have to have strategies to cope. You don't get taught this at medical school. Elsewhere people get diagnosed with PTSD but we tend to just plod on. I know very few emergency department people whose lives haven't been adversely affected by the job in some way or other.

How come I'm getting angry and thinking about work when I'm picking runner beans on a sunny day? Yesterday, we had a particularly harrowing major trauma. Sometimes you just feel so inadequate despite your very best efforts. You might say that heroes only exist in films and comic books but I can promise you they live in the emergency department too.

Some horrible people killed and injured a load of children and some of their parents with a bomb. I wasn't involved – I was on holiday, but my colleagues were. They did what they do best and they did it very well. I was proud of them.

On the ranch, I'm messing about making a small portable mini-greenhouse/propagator affair – it has pointed legs so that it can be knocked into the ground and a curved roof made out of corrugated plastic. The idea is that it can be moved every year as part of the crop rotation. I'm going to grow peas in it next spring. It has it's own guttering which feeds into a water butt. The water butt will contain a hessian sack of comfrey (a superb fertiliser) and will have a tap which feeds back inside to a soak hose. Hence, when the tap is turned on, it will water and feed the peas. When it's raining, it will be self-watering and feeding. When it's not raining and it's dry, the water butt will need topping up with a couple of buckets of water every so often – much quicker and more efficient than using watering cans and adding fertiliser to them.

It's that lovely September weather with the warm lingering embers of a fading summer. *Tempus Fugit* – I'd better get a move on with some of those projects.

18. Painting Snails.

Table, top of ranch. A Tuesday in late September.

It's my birthday and I'm on the ranch sitting at the little table that I made for writing. I'm in demi-shed B. It's ten o'clock in the morning. I brought my little laptop but the fucker won't even switch on. I feel like throwing it across the field like a Frisbee. I'm back to paper and pencil just like when I started. I'm here to write the last chapter.

I often like to sulk and have tantrums on my birthday. I already had my birthday twat tantrum earlier this morning when Louise started characteristically smashing about in the kitchen (which adjoins my chambers) just as I started trying to write. I was up at 6.30.

'You don't give a shit about my book.'

I'm right, she doesn't.

'If you want to read it, you'll have to buy a copy.'

'I don't, and if I did, I'd get it from the library.'

'You are not my muse,' I say.

'You're not my muse either and the neighbours can hear you.' (Apparently they too are writing a book[*]). She made me a lovely breakfast and she'd bought me a beautiful Japanese print.

A balmy September has at last given way to a late autumn as the nights become longer than the days. As ever the English with their love of weather superlatives have had a field day and the weather girls and boys and the headline writers are all at it.

'The longest run of hot September days since granny Cleggthorpe's knickers were nicked off the washing line in 1911.'

It's mild and grey and damp with a haze of ultra-FPD drifting in the breeze. I've had to move back away from the windowless window. The paper was getting damp. I've lit the stove and it's warm and cosy. There's a dog barking in the distance and I can hear the hum of the town. The magpies living in the big hawthorn at the bottom are

---

[*] entitled *The Cunt Next Door*

eyeing me, trying to work out whether I've brought any food that they can steal when I'm not looking. (I haven't).

I've nearly done it. I've almost written a book from birthday to birthday. It's just taken a few more birthdays than I anticipated, that's all.

Here's what really happened.

I did indeed sit down on my birthday a few years ago enthused with the idea of writing a book over twelve months. What's more, I did it. The notion of writing every single day slowly went by the wayside but I continued to write on a regular basis, ending up with a two-inch wad of hand-written A4 – 842 sides. At the end of the year, I was expecting some victorious flourish of literary gushing to finish my tome but it was a miserable anti-climax. I came up here and it was cold, wet and windy. I was fed up. I did my best and wrote a couple of sides then I packed up and went home. I cheated and finished it off the next day, going through the list of goals I'd set myself at the beginning, none of which I'd managed to achieve.

I left it for a while then I read back over some of what I'd written and I just thought what a pile of self-indulgent snivelling shite. I abandoned the idea and put the wad in a drawer and that was that.

My habit of regular writing however was well established and I continued writing little blogs on my record label website using the same theme – allotment ramblings and various anecdotes.

It was probably over a year before I took the wad out of the drawer again and had another look. I began to think that maybe it's not such a bad idea after all and that I should try and see it through – finish what I'd started and all that, so I began again. My original title was going to be *A year in the life of an allotment owner*, but Boff pointed out that it was a crap title because it didn't convey anything about Rock & Roll or medicine. It's become more like *Five years in the life of an allotment owner*.

Some of the original goals were beginning to fall into place. The VINCENT BLACK LIGHTNING records were long finished and I was well on the way with my solo record. I abandoned the idea of calling myself *John Lee Hartley*. I'd just be plain Stephen Hartley (or maybe my full name Stephen John Hartley). I decided to record twelve songs just on my own – live, no overdubs – just my hand-built amp and my beautiful old guitar. It would be a draft record to go with the first draft of the book. I just used two microphones and recorded it in a day. I had over sixty songs to chose from. I chose quieter one's that tied in with the book – they're anecdotal and written from experience so hopefully the book and the record complement each other.

I was very inspired by hearing Leonard Cohen's last interview shortly after he'd died. I've never really been into him, but Louise likes him and Tyler is a big fan. His passion for songwriting and the way he described the value of the songs in almost a religious way gave me inspiration.

Michael Spencer came over from Australia for a visit and we played some music in the back room on New Year's Eve. My brother got back on the drums after a long absence. Bryn played bass and Tyler played a set on the drums too. We also made a couple of quick videos with Notsensibles' Gary on bass – all good fun. Tyler and Michael have similar tastes in music and they got on very well. They both like Scott Walker who I must admit I had to re-evaluate. I'd always considered him too cheesy for my taste. Michael once persuaded me to have a go at Jacques Brel's *Ne me Quitte pas* (translated to *If you go Away* for Scott Walker's English version). I learned it reluctantly.

I had a plan for getting my book published, but after a chance Sunday afternoon at Leeds Central Library, I abandoned that too. Boff was doing a concert there with *The Commoners Choir* and the theme was the value of the printed word and its influence. He asked me to take my letterpress set-up and print a little memento to give out.

Louise and I went and we took two presses – one to print a woodblock and some text in black and the other to print some text in red. We used a Joseph Ames quote: 'Souls dwell in a printer's type.'

Seeing the card come off the presses with a glistening image in shiny black and red ink was quite magical and people were fascinated. I was reminded of a time when I used to do a lot of bookbinding and letterpress printing.

My original plan was to send my book off to agents as I was completing the final touches. For a non-fiction book, you have to send a proposal and a couple of chapters. If I didn't hear anything by the time it was all finished, I would go down the self-publishing route. Then I thought, hold on a minute, I don't know who any of these fuckers are. Do I really want to give 15% to a complete stranger? The establishment tells you that to bring out a book, you need an agent, a publisher, a proofreader, an editor and so on. But hold on boy, I have to do things the hard way – just like I always have done.

It occurred to me that I have everything at home to print and manufacture books – nipping press – guillotine – laser printer. I could possibly make a few copies although it would be mighty time-consuming and labour-intensive. I decided to cut little woodblocks for the chapter beginnings. I had some that I could re-use. In fact the nipping press woodblock that I used at Leeds library is at the beginning of chapter four. I have the naive idea of getting a few copies printed in the hope of getting wider publishing. I also have to realise that I can't always do absolutely everything on my own. It would be better to be able to concentrate on the writing and get experts in the field to do the other bits, but I'm not there yet. For a start, my English isn't good enough to do the proofreading (my brother helped me with it – he also made lots of helpful editing suggestions). It's the same with making a record. It's good to get an outsider to help with the final finishing process.

I kept that old van after all. I used some of the money that my dad left me to get the front end rebuilt by a bloke in The Dirty Old Town. I had the front and roof painted green. I needed a garage and/or workshop to do the rest of the jobs needed for the MOT so I built one on the ranch. It's not exactly a garage. It's a clear plastic roof on legs that provides a minimal shelter. The top bit is raised up to form a kind of mini greenhouse and I've fitted a stove that I bought off my brother. There's a bottle wall at the back with discarded double-glazed window units for windows. It took me six months but it was ready when the van came back – demi-shed D.

My old faded Golf estate was getting very tired and I needed something to get up the ranch whilst the van was off the road. Obviously, there was only one choice – A Land Rover (a traditional green square one – not one of the later uglier ones). I avidly 'studied the form' for a few weeks – crikey, they're expensive (and unreliable and impractical – right up my street). I finally bid on one on ebay – I didn't win it – thank fuck for that.

For once in my life, I do something sensible and buy a NICE car. It's not just nice – it's gorgeous – sleek, fast, arse-warming seats, safe and VERY comfortable. When the van was off the road, I camped in it twice. It's a four-wheel drive and will negotiate the track and the field with graceful ease and aplomb. There are adverts on the internet showing rugged Norsemen driving them across rough terrain and camping in the wilderness. Smithy at work has one and I collectively refer to them as *Smithymobiles*. We have conversations about their boundless merits. He's just got a new one and he points out that once you've had one, you will automatically want another. I think he's right. We're two of the older consultants and he quite likes the fact that I'm the oldest. We have old-twat conversations about the politics of the department and life in general.

One day in summer some nurses from work came to the ranch to film some footage for a video on sepsis. It was a beautiful hot sunny day. We drove the car to the top of the field and played the backing track on the stereo. I filmed it and I had a small cameo role dressed in Boyce's borrowed *Reaper* fancy dress costume. It was good fun. I realised that it's OK to merge work and home life. These are wonderful people and knowing them is a privilege. Sharing good fortune is a big thing in permaculture.

Ruth came to the ranch yesterday with her rescued Sri Lankan street dog Nancy. She only lives up the road. We've known each other many years and we're the best of friends even though we don't see each other that often. She's as close to the bone as me and then some. We can talk about ANYTHING and we do. I gave her one of the first draft copies of the book. She gave me a big confidence-booster by being very complimentary and encouraging – I'd been expecting her to chide me for my bombastic political incorrectness and swearing but she said it was fine. She's the polar opposite of me in terms of being out-going and fearless in public. We were once wandering about once at Beatherder festival and I lost her. I looked up and there she was on the main stage, dancing with the band. Yesterday, amongst other things, we covered death, depression and sex and other stuff far too lurid for general public consumption.

She's been writing poetry for a while (Ruthless Poetry) and has just started writing a blog. It's pretty graphic. It's been well-received so far – particularly by women. I comment that her language sounds very broad-northern and might not necessarily convey her intelligence and intellect. She replies that she doesn't give a fuck any more what people think – she's written it that way because that's how she speaks. She's using a 'stream of consciousness' style where she writes down exactly what she's thinking. I might try that. I suggest breaking it up a bit with paragraphs and maybe a couple of photos. I tell her that I've mentioned her in a later edit of the language chapter in the context of being a woman who doesn't mind using the 'c' word when necessary. I explain that I was going to describe her as a 'staunch feminist' but then decided to use a less dismissible expression. She immediately retorts that it's fine to refer to her as staunch feminist – even better a 'radical feminist'.

Last summer Sam and I built the foundations and low walls for a greenhouse in the field. It's about halfway down and commands the second-best view. You can see both the big hills to the left and the right and the straight mile of the canal framed in the centre. We built a double compost bin on the side with an inward-facing bottle wall. The idea is to fill the bins with rotting compost (which generates a lot of heat) allowing the bottles to act as a radiator to heat the greenhouse. I'm trying to finish it in time for summer – demi-shed C. Elias says I should finish one shed before starting another. He's right, but I needed somewhere to work on the van and I need a greenhouse.

It took me six months to get the van back on the road. I rebuilt the back brakes and I fitted a new wiring loom, adding hazard warning lights. It passed the MOT. Once roadworthy, it typically broke down twice. In fact it ran out of petrol. I didn't realise that the fuel sender was jammed. The fuel gauge was reading half full. I finally found out to how adjust the twin carbs properly and now it's running more sweetly than ever and back on workhorse duties. It's the perfect mascot for a gardening business. In fact we went out in it on Saturday to the *Three Wise Monkeys* in Tod for Fran's birthday (and by default mine and Dewy's too). We took Ann, Taff and Dewy over. There were ten of us in total at the restaurant and we all fitted in the van on the way back. Going slowly round a bend, everyone in the back suddenly screamed. I thought. 'I'm not going that fast.' The side doors had flown open – they weren't shut properly – thankfully no-one fell out.

Never a dull moment in the magic bus. Taff and Louise were on the bench seat in the front with me, swigging a left-over bottle of wine from the restaurant. Taff was fondly recalling the old VW bay window that he and Ann had for many years. They drove it all over Europe when their kids were small. Taff wistfully recounted the numerous times they had broken down and reckoned that a breakdown had occurred on average every hundred miles. Mine's doing a bit better than that at the moment – touch wood.

Flushed with smallholding demi-grandeur, I decided that I needed a tractor. True to form, instead of buying something modern and sensible, I bought a 1954 Ferguson

TEF20 – better known as *the little grey Fergie*. It's not complete madness. They're supposed to be reliable and easy to work on and you can still get all the parts. I came across it after talking to two blokes who were sitting on their restored tractors at the local classic car show. They knew someone who was selling one who lived about ten miles from us. Elias and I went and looked at it and bought it. It's road-registered and the bloke drove it over for us. The whole transaction was by word of mouth. I like that – localisation versus globalisation. I've fitted a roll bar and tidied up a few bits. I bought a cement mixer to run off the power take-off on the back from a farm near Bradford. Louise and I drove over one Sunday morning and picked it up in the van.

The dog is old now. Even when he's not farting he stinks. Still, he's no trouble. He limps a bit and he's getting slow but he keeps going.

Yesterday before Ruth came down, I had one of my 'runabout' mornings. If I'm taking something to the ranch in the van, I make sure I take a full load, so I stock up on sand, cement, timber etc. I called in on Max and Joanne. I was fully expecting Max to have retired by now but he's still doing a bit. We're on the same wavelength. Our conversations have the same baseline refreshing vulgarity that they've always had. I like listening to his Yorkshire dialect. We reminisce about times at the old engineering firm – hiding the boss's glasses – putting an unflushable plastic turd in the managers' toilet. Their new dog takes a liking to me. It's a Shnauser (or however you spell it). We're talking about if we had our time again. I say that I wish I'd realised earlier that I wasn't cut out for being trapped indoors. He makes one of his cheeky expressions in reference to what he wished he'd done more of. Jo raises her eyebrows and makes a deadpan comment. 'Have you not got something to do?' Max replies jokingly.

Their neighbour James is there and he agrees wholeheartedly with the notion of an outdoor livelihood. He's 30 and they've watched him grow up. He's been teaching outdoor stuff in America. Good on him. He too has a VW van – a T4. As I'm leaving, Max and I have a look. He's lined the inside and has a basic fold-out bed – what more does a young gentleman need?

I'd set off on my runabout about 10.30 and as always I'd put woman's hour on the radio (is it one woman? Is it several women? Is it possessive or plural? – Oh how I have struggled with apostrophes and commas – Michael has explained it to me several times but I still keep getting it wrong – reported speech, quotes – it's a nightmare).

I love the juxtaposition of feisty Jane at the beginning of the week and gentle Jenny, with her wonderful mellow voice, at the end of the week. Woman's hour is like Ruth –

they will tackle ANY subject without fear (relating mainly to women obviously). They're talking about problems with sex in marriage then the serial comes on – the programme always finishes with a generally excellent serialised story lasting about fifteen minutes.

Today it's A J Cronin's *The Citadel* which is set in a Welsh mining village. (Maybe I should just have been S J Hartley?) It centres around a newly-arrived young doctor. I said that I don't read much but I have read a few A J Cronin books. Born in 1896, he was a doctor who became a writer.

In the serial, The older doctor – a real firebrand who is fighting against the gross social inequality (nothing like me – honest) is planning to blow up a dangerous sewer that is responsible for a number of typhoid outbreaks. The young newly-arrived doctor got into medical school from an unlikely background and guess which one he went too? St Andrews. He gets reluctantly involved in the plot and floats the ignited dynamite down the sewer in tin cans.

Apparently Cronin worked with Aneurin Bevan at one point, and the book (with its radical ideas) is credited with having a hand in the creation of the NHS. The serial finishes and the announcer says '... and the series was produced in Salford by Gary Brown.' Well it's obviously not the same Gary Brown as NOTSENSIBLES bass player, but still a weird little coincidence. (Salford is Salford by the way – it's NOT Manchester).

I'm nearly there. I keep thinking of bits that I've forgotten to include. I have to stop somewhere though. I've got the bug now – for writing that is – maybe I'll write another. Hold on a minute though, I've got to sell this one first – says me who couldn't sell water in a desert.

There's something uniquely comforting about driving an old tractor round a field. Growing plants feels good. Building guitar amps feels good. Cutting woodblocks and printing with letterpress feels good. Making records feels good.

Years ago, when the kids were little, times were difficult. I was doing seven twelve-hour nights a week sandwiched between a three-hour commute. One sunny day there was a brief moment of peace when I realised that I needed to appreciate the present. The kids were finding snails in the little bit of frontage outside the house then painting them. They were completely absorbed in painting little colourful patterns on their shells and I realised that heaven really is in the ordinary.

Appendix 1

BMJ. 2004 Dec 4; 329(7478): 1341.
PMCID: PMC534852

A memorable teacher

The philosopher DJ

Stephen Hartley, specialist registrar in emergency medicine

I failed all my A level exams the first time round, mainly because I had better things to do. I played guitar in a punk band, and I was busy playing gigs and making records.

Our first gig was at the local youth club. Our second was at Band on The Wall in Manchester, where the owner of a local record label offered to release a single for us. Punk had just smashed its way on to the music scene, and – as with all new and interesting music before and since – the disc jockey John Peel avidly championed it. He played our first single and gave us a session. Subsequently, he played our album and further three singles and was always supportive and encouraging.

For me, and countless others with a passion for music, his evening radio programmes were an intensely important part of our lives. He was famous for breaking countless bands and introducing new music to his listeners. What really mattered, though, was the bit in between the records – the sound of his voice and his wry commentary on all aspects of his daily life. Over the years, we shared with him his family's ups and downs. We knew the names of his children and his pets. Later we learnt how he coped with his wife Sheila's cerebral aneurysm and his own diabetes.

I came to medicine late in life and sometimes struggled to balance my love of music with work commitments. Punk wasn't just about music – it was also about fierce independence, and a healthy anti-establishment view. At times I wondered whether I was suited to working within such a rigid structure as the NHS.

One day, on my birthday, I emailed John Peel, telling him that I'd been listening to his programmes since the age of 14. I mentioned that I'd once played in a punk band and that I was now a doctor. He read out my email in his usual kind way and at the end pointed out that I'd neglected to mention the name of the band. As chance would have it, the band's former drummer was also listening. He emailed our band name to John, who, minutes later, announced this on the airwaves, adding that I should "be singing it from the rooftops." This not only made my day but also helped me to realise that it's OK to be a doctor and play in a rock and roll band. In fact, medicine is so diverse that it has its own rock and roll (emergency medicine), cabaret (general practice), and death metal (orthopaedics).

John Peel didn't just teach us about music. He taught us how to place passionate enthusiasm and fierce individualism into the context of ordinary life, and, now that he's gone, we're realising how much he taught us about kindness, compassion, and humility.

Appendix 2

IAQs – Infrequently asked Questions.

Favourite film: What fucker said that? Withnail and I of course. A sub-section of each generation (including my lads and their mates) know all the lines off by heart. 'If I medicine you man, you'd think a brain tumour was a birthday present.' 'Am I the farmer? Of course I'm the fucking farmer.' It's my brother's favourite film too and he's visited the cottage that some of it is filmed in. Virtually every line is pure gold – there are too many to mention. Perhaps my favourite is, 'Shove it up your arse and fuck off while you're doing it.' I've fantasised about including it in a twat letter, or at least alluding to it - 'Sir, I will leave it to your imagination to decide which line from *Withnail and I* most appropriately fits the situation.'

When the lads were teenagers, herding them up into the van after gigs sometimes took ages. They often took the piss out of me by barking the 'Get in the back of the van!' line. Other gems include 'Terrible cunt' and 'We want the finest wines available to humanity, we want them here and we want them now!' Ah,...the paragon of animals.

Favourite Book: I hardly read books. Journey to Ixtlan by Carlos Castaneda. I adore Steinbeck's Sweet Thursday and Cannery row. My aunt Christine is in a book club and coincidentally, she recently gave a talk on Cannery Row.

Favourite radio programme: Woman's Hour – I listen to it on the way to work.

Favourite year for music: 1969 – there's all-sorts from 1969: the best of the sixties; Northern Soul; R&B; Ska – someone wrote a book on a similar theme but they chose 1971.

Favourite radio presenters: John Peel, Jennifer Murray, Jane Garvey, Marc Riley.

Favourite TV presenter: Kirsty Wark. She had Rage against The Machine on The Late Show before they were famous. In the wake of faux patriotism surrounding Brexit, some pompous dick wrote into Newsnight suggesting that they play out with *God Save The Queen*. 'Happy to oblige', Said Kirsty at the end of the programme before finishing with a live Sex Pistols version. I admired her for that. Pure class.

Favourite guitars: 1964 Gretsch Tennessean, 1964 Hofner Verithin,

Favourite single: Too many to mention but Swing Easy by The Soul Vendors; Cry before I Go by John Lee Hooker; Going Down for the Last Time by Ronnie Keaton and the Oceanliners are up there. I'm always interested in the recorded sound and production of records and my gold standard is *Honky Tonk Woman* by The Stones. The production, the dynamics – everything about it is impeccable. It was recorded at Olympic Studios in Barnes and was released on 9th of July 1969 – the day after Brian Jones' death. It's the first single to feature Mick Taylor although the magnificent guitar playing that dominates the song is Keith through and through. If I could achieve any recorded sound, then that would be it. Sadly a lot of the classic English studios are gone now – swept away by the digital age.

Favourite guitarist: Hendrix is up there but my favourite from that era is Peter Green. He had that exquisite understated tone. John Mayall once paid for him to have some recording time at Decca studios and he recorded four songs with Mick Fleetwood on drums and John McVie on bass. He named one of the songs (an instrumental) *Fleetwood Mac* after the rhythm section and that was the birth of the band. One of my favourite bits of guitar playing ever is on *First Train Home* from the same session – the phrasing and tone are utterly exquisite – unsurpassed.

Others include Carl Perkins, Cliff Gallup (played on Gene Vincent's first two albums – the finest rockabilly player of all in my opinion), Scotty Moore of course and Steve Cropper. I saw Steve Cropper play at The Grand in Clitheroe and I'm glad I did. He was great. He played loads of his classic riffs, dotted with charming anecdotes. I was thinking 'I'm in the same room as someone who has been in the same room as Otis Redding.' He played on countless Stax records and has the most wonderful all-round rhythmic style. One of my favourite tracks with him on it is Wilson Pickett's version of *Sugar Sugar* – he plays the most delicious little riff right at the end. The spiky riff on Eddie Floyd's *Knock on Wood* is magnificent.

Favourite album: For years I've had a tradition of putting on an album when we sit down for our Sunday dinner. I don't buy them much these days mainly because the shelf space to the left of where I'm writing is jam-packed and there's no room for more. There are too many to mention but one that I've probably played the most is Aretha Franklin's greatest hits. I got John Lee Hooker's Urban Blues for Christmas and that's great. My favourite relatively recent album is *Brightly Painted One* by Tiny Ruins on Bella Union. It's very gentle and mellow – great for playing at the end of the day before bedtime.

Favourite guitar riff: – played by Scotty Moore on *Mystery Train*. It's a simple but masterful phrase, bolstered with echo. On the one hand it's ridiculously simple, yet it's extremely difficult to play. It's syncopated and played in a claw-hammer style with the thumb playing alternating octave bass notes. It moves between an E and an A chord. The whole essence of the riff is the steam train power and regularity of the bass notes. There are loads of internet vids showing you how to play it but none of them get it quite right. Scotty had lots of magnificent similar riffs. Once you've mastered one, the rest are easier.

Favourite Family listening: We were far too liberal as parents. Whilst other small children were watching *Rugrats,* mine were watching *South Park* and *League of Gentlemen.* One artist that we all liked was *Eminen* and his first three albums were standard listening in the car – wonderfully politically incorrect, yet so incisive and insightful. Genius. When *Slim Shady* came out, Rachel was eleven, Elias was seven and Sam was five. They all used to sing *Daddy's Gone Crazy* at me. My favourite track is *Business.* It's a clever tribute to Marshall and Dre's friendship, using a Batman and Robin analogy – To the rapmobile. Let's go.

Favourite food: Toast.

Favourite garden: I don't really time to visit other gardens but I did spend a full day in The Chelsea Physic a few years ago and absolutely loved it – it's been there since 1673.

Favourite word: ... probably obvious by now. *Exquisite* is up there too.

There must be loads more *LAQs* but I can't think of them just now.